HOW'

Genera

HOW TO STUDY A CHARLES DICKENS NOVEL

How to Study
Series editors: John Peck and Martin Coyle

HOW TO STUDY A
CHARLES DICKENS NOVEL

Keith Selby

palgrave
macmillan

Published by
PALGRAVE
Houndmills, Basingstoke, Hampshire RG21 6XS and
175 Fifth Avenue, New York, N.Y. 10010
Companies and representatives throughout the world

PALGRAVE is the new global academic imprint of
St. Martin's Press LLC Scholarly and Reference Division and
Palgrave Publishers Ltd (formerly Macmillan Press Ltd).

ISBN 0–333–46728–0

This book is printed on paper suitable for recycling and
made from fully managed and sustained forest sources.

A catalogue record for this book is available
from the British Library.

Printed and bound in Great Britain by Antony Rowe, Eastbourne

Contents

General editors' preface

EVERYBODY who studies literature, either for an examination or simply for pleasure, experiences the same problem: how to understand and respond to the text. As every student of literature knows, it is perfectly possible to read a book over and over again and yet still feel baffled and at a loss as to what to say about it. One answer to the problem, of course, is to accept someone else's view of the text, but how much more rewarding it would be if you could work out your own critical response to any book you choose or are required to study.

The aim of this series is to help you develop your critical skills by offering practical advice about how to read, understand and analyse literature. Each volume provides you with a clear method of study so that you can see how to set about tackling texts on your own. While the authors of each volume approach the problem in a different way, every book in the series attempts to provide you with some broad ideas about the kind of texts you are likely to be studying and some broad ideas about how to think about literature; each volume then shows you how to apply these ideas in a way which should help you construct your own analysis and interpretation. Unlike most critical books, therefore, the books in this series do not convey someone else's thinking about a text, but encourage you to think about a text for yourself.

Each book is written with an awareness that you are likely to be preparing for an examination, and therefore practical advice is given not only on how to understand and analyse literature, but also on how to organise a written response. Our hope is that although these books are intended to serve a practical purpose, they may also enrich your enjoyment of literature by making you a more confident reader, alert to the interest and pleasure to be derived from literary texts.

John Peck
Martin Coyle

Acknowledgements

I SHOULD LIKE to acknowledge the help I have received from John Peck, who first taught me how to read and understand a novel, and who has guided me so generously through the writing of this book. I am particularly grateful to my wife Susan for her encouragement and support, and to my daughter Rebekah, who told me to get on with it. Finally, I should like to thank Martin Coyle for his painstaking and extremely helpful editorial guidance.

For my parents

1

Introduction:
reading a Dickens novel

THE CHANCES are that, if you are studying English at school, college or university, you will have to read quite a few novels. While they are easy and enjoyable to read, however, novels are notoriously difficult to write about. For example, while you might enjoy reading the thousand or so pages of Dickens's *Dombey and Son,* you would probably be hard-pressed to write a good, thousand-word critical response to the novel. One of the major problems of all novels, in fact, is that they seem to resist our efforts to analyse them critically.

This difficulty seems to be much greater in the case of Dickens's novels. Because most of his novels are fairly long, it seems hard to recall them and decide which bits you should be commenting on. One way round this problem, of course, is to turn to critical books for help, but these may merely add to your problems. Some critics will tell you that Dickens's greatness is to be found in his comic writing and in his genius as a creator of caricatures; others will suggest that Dickens should be regarded as a social reformer, his stories acting as a sugar coating on the moral pill he wants his readers to swallow; others still will tell you that he is concerned with the effects of Victorian economic principles on the life of the individual. What might trouble you most of all about such ideas is the way they differ from your perceptions of the novel you are studying, or the difficulty of seeing their relevance when the only thing you remember about *Hard Times,* for example, is that some of the characters are funny. At this stage it is all too easy to begin to believe that the critic must be right, and to forget the enjoyment that your reading of the novel gave you.

This is also the point at which many students give up trying to shape their own response to the novel they have read, because they can see little connection between their own experience of the book and the kind of things that appear to be central in criticism.

Yet most students know that studying English is only going to be really worthwhile if they can formulate their own view of a text. The major aim of this book is to show you how to move from your reading of one of Dickens's novels to shaping your own response to that novel. A central point, which will be stressed all the time, is that the best way to build a critical response is to start with a few clear, simple ideas about the novel as a whole and to use these ideas to direct and shape all your subsequent thinking. To do this, however, you must first learn how to read a novel in an analytical way, and to identify what the novel is about.

Seeing what a novel is about

On a first reading of a novel you are likely to be so absorbed in the details of the story that you might fail to perceive a larger pattern at work in the text. Yet it is precisely this sense of a larger pattern that you need to establish when you begin to think about the novel critically. This book is about how to move beyond that initial bewildered response.

The first point to grasp about novels in general is that novelists tend to return to the same issues and situations time and again. Clearly, a strong sense of the story being told, and an ability to reduce that to a few basic points, is a fundamental first step in beginning to get a sense of the larger pattern at work in a novel.

The second point is to remind yourself that all literature is concerned with some kind of opposition or conflict. You have probably noticed that poems tend to employ a basic opposition to draw attention to the problems that the poet is concerned with. This can be any kind of conflict or opposition at all: day is opposed by night, light by dark, youth by old age, good by bad, right by wrong, and so on. These oppositions are all around us, and many people argue that it is through these opposites that we begin to make sense of the world. Certainly, in a novel, the novelist tends to pattern events, characters and settings in such a way that they are opposed with one another, thereby dramatising and illustrating the conflicts at the centre of the novel.

The broadest pattern that can be observed in a novel is of some kind of conflict between society and one or more individuals within that society. In Dickens's novels, as we shall see, the conflict tends to be shifted a little, to the conflict or opposition between the world of money, greed, lust and desire, on the one hand, and a sense of natural goodness and love, on the other. But we shall be looking at this in much more detail later. For the moment, the second thing to grasp about novels in general is that some kind of conflict resides at their centre. If we can be sure about the general nature of this conflict, then we can begin to see how all the details of the novel form part of an overall pattern, and so begin to produce a coherent critical response to the novel as a whole.

The final point to remember about novels for the moment is that they begin on the first page and end on the last. What happens between the first and last pages is the story. This may seem self-evidently true and hardly worth stating, but the first and last pages can tell us a great deal about the way in which the story will work, and how it has worked. The opening pages of the novel are going to establish most of the details and conflicts of the rest of the novel. The ending of the novel is the culmination of all the events and details of the story. The more important of these two moments for our purpose is going to be the beginning, since it is there that the major conflicts and tensions of the novel will be most apparent.

To summarise briefly: first, *it is important to have a good, strong sense of the story being told and to be able to reduce that to a few major points*; secondly, *it is important to recognise the basic conflict or tension between opposites which forms the core of the novel*; and, finally, *the best place to locate those oppositions is likely to be in the first few paragraphs of the novel*, since it is here that the conflict at the heart of the novel is going to be most apparent.

It is these three steps which mark out the process I am going to describe in this book, and which provide a useful critical framework for analysing a novel. What you will notice about this process is that it starts from simple ideas of what a novel is about, moves down to the details on the page, and then allows us to move back again to the larger, broader concerns and aspects of the novel as a whole. The logic of this approach is that it makes you work from the text and draw all your evidence from a close analysis of the details contained in the words on the page. How exactly this can be applied to specific novels will be demonstrated in the chapters given over to each novel I discuss. For the moment, it will help if you can remember the three points discussed above. The major one is the notion of a conflict or tension of some kind. What I want to do now is to consider further the nature of the conflict or tension commonly found in Dickens's novels.

The conflict in Dickens's novels

As I mentioned above, the broadest pattern that can be observed in a novel is of some kind of conflict between society and one or more individuals within that society. In Dickens's novels, this conflict tends to be expressed as a tension between two opposed ideas: on the one hand, we find a broad panorama of lust, greed, desire, show and affectation, and on the other, a sense of natural simplicity of spirit, of goodness and love for our fellow humans. This opposition can be simplified even further to the basic conflict between money on the one side, and love on the other.

Many of the reasons why Dickens concentrated on the opposition or conflict between money and love can be found in the nature of Victorian society itself. The Victorian period was a time of rapid social, technological, cultural and economic change. Dickens, who was born in 1812 and died in 1870, lived through this period of change, and he was, like other Victorian writers, acutely aware that he was living through a period of transition which would change the whole fabric and structure of society. What was at the root of all this change was the development of machinery, which meant that more could be produced, more cheaply and more efficiently. This in turn meant that more could be sold and more profit could be made.

But what the Victorians were forced to recognise was that all these changes brought about by the development of machinery were not minor or cosmetic improvements or conveniences. Some of these mechanical conveniences might have appeared trivial enough. According to one nineteenth-century writer and commentator, Thomas Carlyle, the Victorians had steam-driven machines for mincing cabbages and hatching chicks. But they also had the railway, which replaced the stagecoach; factories, which replaced the artisan and cottage industries; steamships, which replaced the old sailing ships; the steam press, which replaced the hand press; the telegraph, which replaced the messenger. What all these changes meant was that things were moving faster and faster, more and more was being produced, society was becoming more and more complex. One of the things which fascinated Dickens and other Victorian writers was what effect all this change would have on the inner life of the individual, and on the relations between individuals.

The reason for this interest is simple enough. Victorian society was a complex world of change, of production and economic power, apparently with no place in it for love. The society it had replaced had been (in theory at least) a stable society in which there had been a a natural relationship between individuals based upon love. But, in a society based upon the economic principles of production, some people will become rich by exploiting the talents, the labour and the weaknesses of others. Some, the particularly vulnerable – such as the old, the infirm, and children – will fall by the wayside. These characters are capable of offering love and a simplicity of spirit, but how can the rich respond to them, poisoned as they are by the loveless world of change, economic production and money?

It is this conflict between money and love which forms the core of Dickens's novels. What this conflict usually reveals is that the people who have the greatest love for their fellow humans are also the ones who are most hurt by the world of money, simply because money is power. In Dickens's novels, the people who possess most money and most power seem incapable of love, whereas the people who *are* capable of love are very often both poor and powerless.

This is a potentially gloomy vision of the world, because it suggests that the good and the poor will always suffer at the hands of the bad and the rich. And yet, as we know, Dickens is a *comic* novelist. He is in fact probably the finest comic novelist in English literature. How, though, can Dickens's novels be described as comic when his view of the world is potentially such a gloomy one? To answer this question we need to think a little more about comedy.

Comedy in Dickens's novels consists of laughing at characters trapped in difficult situations. People are commonly seen as types, illustrating particular human traits – traits such as greed or lust. As a result, these human weaknesses are exaggerated to comic proportions and emerge as funny. Society itself is seen as a paper-thin veneer, barely covering man's basic desires of greed, lust and self-interest. This kind of comedy is concerned to draw our attention to the absurdity of human affectation and social pretensions, because it suggests that people tend to be motivated more by self-interest than love; it draws attention also to the darker, irrational desires lurking just behind the social façade. Such a view of the world is not only a potentially gloomy one, but also an extremely disturbing one, since there seems nothing of any permanence to hold on to when society is presented as little more than an elaborate charade. One of the odd things about comic novels, then, and one of the most difficult things to grasp, is that they are very serious novels, presenting a disturbing view of how society conducts itself.

In Dickens's novels, all this probing of society and its institutions, along with the probing of the dark impulses that motivate humans, arises from the basic conflict between money and love. What we can expect to find at the centre of Dickens's novels is a presentation of the experiences of one or more characters caught between these two worlds of money and of love, and of the kinds of demands that the world of money puts on the individual in his or her relationships with other people. We can expect to find these situations presented comically, but this does not detract from the novel's seriousness. The basic frame, then, on which to build an analysis of Dickens's novels, is that of the conflict between the world of money and self-interest and the sense of a natural goodness and love in human beings.

Putting a novel back together again

An awareness of this money-*versus*-love conflict in Dickens's novels should give you a firm foundation on which you can build your reading of a particular novel. It should help you make sense of the incidents which make up the story and help you in your interpretation of particular scenes and details. If you always look for a money-*versus*-love conflict, this should help you begin interpreting any scene or detail in any of Dickens's novels. What might concern you is that using this idea might seem to limit your interpretation, but this should not be the case. What I am talking about is a very basic pattern in Dickens's fiction; it is how you fill out this pattern that will make your reading of a Dickens novel distinctive, and all kinds of readings can be built on this solid foundation.

Sometimes, however, rather than being left to pursue your own line through a novel, you might be called upon to consider a particular topic. In preparing for an examination, for example, you might be asked to discuss such issues as Dickens's presentation of class differences, or the way in which some people seem to be doomed victims in his stories, or his presentation of childhood. All too often students make the mistake of regarding such things as totally disparate topics, writing about them as if they are quite separate aspects of a novel. The point to appreciate here is that such topics interrelate and are simply aspects of the total pattern of the work. The best way to approach such topics is to investigate them in the light of a money-*versus*-love opposition. This will provide you with a way of focusing your impressions, and a way of relating one aspect of the text to all your other ideas about the novel.

Consider, for example, Dickens's interest in childhood. Far too often students write as if Dickens just happened to have a curious, nostalgic obsession with childhood. And published criticism may not be much help here either, as this tends to relate Dickens's presentation of childhood to his own privations during early childhood, and particularly to the period he spent as an eleven-year-old working at Warren's Blacking Company for six shillings a week. Such details might seem interesting, but they do not appear very helpful to an analysis of the *theme* of childhood in a novel. Looked at from the money-*versus*-love opposition, however, it is possible to see how Dickens's interest in and presentation of childhood fits into the larger pattern of his novels as a whole, for the child is traditionally representative of innocence, and this innocence parallels the innocent simplicity which opposes the adult world of greed, lust, show and affectation – the world of money. The idea of childhood, which is a period free from the demands of money, ties in with the notion of innocence and a natural love for our fellow humans. It also links up with the further idea of the doomed victim, since the child is powerless to influence the world around him or her, and so becomes its victim. Clearly, topics interrelate on many levels, and are not the separate or distinct areas they at first appear to be. Dickens's interest in childhood, therefore, is just one of the ways in which he brings to life in his works his larger vision of a constant battle between money and love, and between society and the individual.

In subsequent chapters I hope to explain how other aspects of Dickens's novels can be approached in a similar way, working from the same basic idea. At the moment, however, it is quite possible that the last few paragraphs struck you as rather abstract, since they anticipate issues that the rest of the book will explore. Let me, therefore, return to the main point that I want to get across here. There is a recurrent pattern in Dickens's novels which can be described as a tension between money and love. This is the basic, fundamental conflict that underlies all Dickens's novels, and can be used, as you will see in the following chapters, as the springboard for building a coherent, analytical comment on his fiction.

Analysing a novel

So far I have talked about the standard pattern in Dickens's fiction. In discussing a novel, however, you are primarily concerned with capturing and conveying your sense of the unique and special qualities of that work. The following chapters of this book illustrate how to explore a text in this way. The novels considered are those which are generally considered to be some of Dickens's major works. Obviously, I cannot discuss every Dickens novel, as that would require several more books. But don't be put off if I do not discuss the particular novel you are interested in. The steps in an analysis remain the same, no matter which of Dickens's novels you want to study. In each chapter I start with ideas about the standard pattern of Dickens's novels. Then I analyse the opening paragraph or so from the novel, to establish the precise nature of the conflict at work in that particular novel. Then, with the information gleaned from this analysis, I look closely at several passages from the rest of the novel to establish the way in which the novel presents its major concerns and interests.

This is probably the most important thing to grasp about an actual method of working on a text. Indeed, the whole of this book can be reduced to one simple formula: *look at the novel with a clear idea of the tension likely to be at the heart of the work, and then look closely at the opening and several other passages.* This approach makes sure that your ideas are clear from the outset and forces you to focus on the text itself. There might seem something too simple about just focusing on a few scenes from a long novel, but it is the case that such detailed focusing will help you write far better criticism than if you attempt to discuss too much.

As you read the following chapters, do try to remember that I am primarily concerned to illustrate a method of how *you* can work on the text of a Dickens novel. Try selecting and discussing scenes yourself: the moment you do this you should discover how enjoyable and rewarding working on the text on your own can be.

It might be that you want only to read the chapter about the novel you are studying, but you could find it useful to read this book as a whole. The reason for saying this is that I cannot cover every aspect of Dickens in every chapter, so it may well be that issues which are central to the novel you are studying are in fact discussed elsewhere.

Even if I cannot persuade you to read all the chapters, however, it will certainly be a good idea to read the next chapter, on *Hard Times*, as it is here that I explain most fully the method for working on a text that this book as a whole employs and illustrates.

2

Hard Times

I Constructing an overall analysis

Hard Times was first published in weekly serial form between April and August 1854, and comes just about half way through Dickens's writing career. Because of this, critics have often seen *Hard Times* as not truly 'Dickensian': it lacks the sentimentality, jollity and grotesquery of the earlier novels, yet is not really as serious and probing as the later 'social' novels. But, instead of offering any further introductory comments about *Hard Times*, it will be better if I begin straightaway with the method of analysing a novel that I am going to use throughout this book.

1 *After reading the novel, think about the story and what kind of pattern you can see in the text*

Thomas Gradgrind is an important citizen of Coketown, an imaginary industrial town in the north of England. He has two children, Tom and Louisa, and brings them up according to his belief in practical necessity, denying them all imaginative or emotional outlets. Gradgrind adopts Sissy Jupe, after her father – a performer in Sleary's circus – deserts her. Some years later Gradgrind marries his daughter to Josiah Bounderby, a local bank-owner and manufacturer. Louisa never loves Bounderby, but does love her brother, Tom, and this is part of the reason why she marries, for Tom is employed in Bounderby's bank, and she thinks that by marrying Bounderby she will increase Tom's chances of promotion. But Tom is an idle waster, and eventually robs the bank, trying to place the blame on an innocent factory-hand, Stephen Blackpool. In the meantime, a young, unscrupulous politician, James Harthouse, visits Coketown and tries to seduce Louisa. This experience suddenly awakens Louisa to the fact that she abhors Bounderby, and she runs to her father for protection. This likewise brings Gradgrind to his senses, and he is forced to recognise the foolishness of his beliefs about practical necessity being more important than the emotions.

In the meantime, suspicion for the bank robbery shifts from Blackpool to Tom, and he is speedily bundled out of the country with the assistance of Sleary's circus performers. Blackpool, having been sacked from Bounderby's factory, and now working in another town some sixty miles off, hears that he is suspected of the bank robbery and attempts to walk to Coketown to prove his innocence. But he falls into a disused mineshaft on the way, and, although discovered some days later by Sissy Jupe and his only friend, Rachael, he dies from his injuries. Bounderby continues to live in his bank with his housekeeper, the detestable Mrs Sparsit, and dies of a fit in Coketown High Street five years later, while the sisterly bond between Louisa and Sissy grows ever stronger over the years, with Louisa doting on Sissy's children. Louisa herself, though, is never to remarry.

As you start to think about this story, bear in mind what I said in the previous chapter about the conflict in Dickens's novels between money and love. Before you go any further, try thinking about how you can see this conflict at work in the main characters in the novel. One thing that you might well conclude from your reading of the novel is that there is indeed a vast difference between the people with money – such as Gradgrind and Bounderby – and the people without money – such as Sleary and Sissy Jupe. Money, or the lack of it, is at the centre of the story, and it is the desire for power which money brings that provides the climax to the story. Tom attempts to steal money from Bounderby's bank, because in stealing that money he hopes he will then possess the kind of power already possessed by Bounderby, his employer, and by his father. What you might spot, too, is how money, and the power that it brings, is inevitably corrupting and causes the suffering of innocent people: Blackpool dies as a direct result of Tom robbing the bank, and Louisa sells herself to Bounderby in the hope that this will benefit Tom's career. Money, we see, not only physically controls people's lives (by forcing them to work in dangerous factories, to live in squalid houses), but also corrupts the emotions – Louisa prostitutes herself to Bounderby's money and power, until shocked into recognising the importance of love and her emotions.

In *Hard Times*, then, we can say the central conflict is located in the opposition between the world of money, affectation and self-interest (represented by Bounderby and Gradgrind), and the world of love and a natural simplicity of spirit (represented by Sleary's circus). Between these two extremes are the children and innocents – Tom, Louisa, Sissy, Stephen Blackpool – who all have the potential to partake of the virtues of Sleary's circus world, but who are all made to suffer under Gradgrind's and Bounderby's beliefs about the value of practical necessity. Dickens, it could be said, is focusing on the corrupting power of money, and the way in which it can poison both the physical and the emotional parts of people's lives. This might seem a lot to deduce from a simple outline of the story, but, if you think in terms of how Dickens's novels always present us with a conflict between money and love, this should help you in detecting a pattern in any of his novels.

It may help if we stand back here and look at what I have done so far. I have tried to get at the issues at the heart of the novel by thinking in terms of the basic conflict between the world of money and the world of love. Obviously, though, you should not just accept my overall impression of the novel: try to apply the idea of an opposition to your own summary of *Hard Times*, defining your own sense of the issues involved. What you should discover is that in your first look at the novel you can see an overall opposition and it is this which will give your analysis a firm base to start from.

2   *Analyse the opening paragraph or two of the novel and try to build on the ideas you have established so far*

Once you have established some sense of an overall pattern you can move on to working out a more detailed view of the novel. The best way to achieve this is to focus on small areas of the text: you will not only be illuminating these particular passages but also gaining a more confident understanding of the novel as a whole. But how do you choose appropriate passages for discussion? Well, the best place to start is at the beginning because, as I said in the previous chapter, it is at the beginning of the novel that the novel's concerns and interests are likely to be most apparent. Here are the opening paragraphs of *Hard Times* (page references relate to the Penguin edition, 1979):

'Now what I want is, Facts. Teach these boys and girls nothing but Facts. Facts alone are wanted in life. Plant nothing else, and root out everything else. You can only form the minds of reasoning animals upon Facts: nothing else will ever be of any service to them. This is the principle on which I bring up my own children, and this is the principle on which I bring up these children. Stick to Facts, sir!'

The scene was a plain, bare, monotonous vault of a school-room, and the speaker's square forefinger emphasised his observations by underscoring every sentence with a line on the schoolmaster's sleeve. The emphasis was helped by the speaker's square wall of a forehead, which had its eyebrows for its base, while his eyes found commodious cellarage in two dark caves, overshadowed by the wall. (p. 47)

You now have a passage to talk about, but what do you say about it? Sometimes you might know exactly what you want to say about such a passage, but if you are unsure it is always a good idea to tackle the passage systematically. Try following this sequence of steps.

(a) *Search for an opposition or tension within the passage.*
(b) *Analyse the details of the passage, relating them to the opposition already noted.*
(c) *Try to say how the passage relates to the novel as a whole.*
(d) *Search for anything distinctive about the passage, particularly in the area of style, which you have not already noted.*

This set of steps underlies the analyses of all the extracts discussed in this book, but it is only in this chapter that I label each step. Setting yourself this set of tasks, even when you are talking about a piece of text that you think you already know well, will always help you to organise your response. In addition, it will help you to direct your thinking in a purposeful way rather than floundering around in a sea of vague impressions.

(a) *Search for an opposition or tension within the passage.* If we look at the passage above, it can be argued that (a) the tension in the piece is between the coldness of rational thinking and the ideas of freedom and natural growth. The first paragraph introduces the idea that Thomas Gradgrind brings up his own children – who we later discover are Tom and Louisa – on a diet of bare facts, and this denies much that we normally associate with the freedom of childhood, a time normally not of facts, but of imagination and freedom from the concerns of adulthood. As against our normal impressions of childhood, therefore, we have the adult world of rational facts being imposed upon it, and this will have a deadening effect on the children.

(b) *Analyse the details of the passage, relating them to the opposition already noted.* The details in the passage help to convey this sense of the deadening effects of facts upon the imagination. The room in which Thomas Gradgrind speaks is described as if it were a mortuary or grave rather than a place of imaginative learning. The schoolroom is a 'bare, monotonous vault', and even Gradgrind's face is described in terms reminiscent of the grave: 'his eyes found commodious cellarage in two dark caves'. On the other hand, the 'planting' of these facts will 'root out everything else' – that is, all the imaginative aspects that we normally associate with childhood. And so we find a general conflict between what we as readers associate with childhood, and what the speaker, Thomas Gradgrind, is imposing upon it.

(c) *Try to say how the passage relates to the novel as a whole.* The assumption you have to make in looking at a passage is that it will reflect the larger concerns of the novel. When you look at an extract, therefore, you must step back and relate it to the novel as a whole, trying to sum up what the passage has added to your overall impression. What you might conclude from this passage, for example, is that in this novel we have a basic conflict between adults and children, and this represents a difference in the way in which the world is perceived. On the side of the adults we find facts, and on the side of the children we find the imagination. This has wider implications also, for on the side of the imagination there is love and a general simplicity of spirit – such as we find in Sleary and the circus performers – and on the side of facts there is the obsession with money, greed and self-interest – such as we find in Gradgrind, and, more particularly, in Bounderby. It is an obsession, moreover, which these characters are attempting to *impose* on childhood and the imagination.

(d) *Search for anything distinctive about the passage, particularly in the area of style, which you have not already noted.* The final step in looking at a passage is to take a close look at the style, but I am going to ignore this for the moment as I want to conclude this section by summing up what you should be trying to do as you turn to the text. That is really quite straightforward: you should be trying to flesh out and develop your initial ideas so that you are starting to build a fuller sense of the novel. For example, I began with an overall sense of an opposition between the world of money and the world of love. But already I have started to refine this and fill it out by seeing how the world of money is linked with facts and conformity, whereas the world of love is associated with childhood and imagination. This helps to make me much more clear about the novel as a whole.

3   *Select a second passage for discussion*

Each additional passage you consider should add to your overall impression: keep on asking yourself, what can I now say about this novel that I did not know before? The best way to choose further passages for discussion is to select those scenes which have stayed most vividly in your memory. The most striking of these scenes, to my mind, because it represents such a contrast with the imaginative world of Sleary's circus, is the first description we have of Coketown:

> It was a town of red brick, or of brick that would have been red if the smoke and ashes would have allowed it; but, as matters stood, it was a town of unnatural red and black, like the painted face of a savage. It was a town of machinery and tall chimneys, out of which interminable serpents of smoke trailed themselves for ever and ever, and never got uncoiled. It had a black canal in it, and a river that ran purple with ill-smelling dye, and vast piles of building full of windows where there was a rattling and a trembling all day long, and where the piston of the steam-engine worked monotonously up and down, like the head of an elephant in a state of melancholy madness. It contained many large streets all very like one another, and many small streets still more like one another, inhabited by people equally like one another, who all went in and out at the same hours, with the same sound upon the same pavements, to do the same work, and to whom every day was the same as yesterday and tomorrow, and every year the counterpart of the last and the next. (p. 65)

(a) *Search for an opposition or a tension within the passage.* The major opposition in this passage has to do with the way in which the natural world and the unnatural are offset against each other. This relates directly to the central opposition in Dickens's work between the world of money and self-interest on the one hand and the world of love and simplicity of spirit on the other. In the above passage, of course, the only society being described is that of Coketown itself (the world of money), but it is described in such a way as to suggest its effects upon the natural world (the world of love and simplicity of spirit). There is a sense of violence being done, of frenetic activity, of imprisonment and enforced drudgery and routine, and this clearly contrasts with our sense of a simpler, humane society – the type of society represented by Sleary's circus.

(b) *Analyse the details of the passage, relating them to the opposition already noted.* This opposition is reflected in the imagery used to describe Coketown. Although it is 'a town of machinery', a phrase which tells us that this is a society of mechanisation and mass-production, the machinery itself is ironically likened to an animal from the natural world: 'where the piston of the steam-engine worked monotonously up and down, like the head of an elephant in a state of melancholy madness'. That the work of the piston is likened to the power of an enslaved elephant tells us further that the power which drives the new, mechanised society is not only more powerful than the old, natural society, but also destructive: the imaginary elephant is put into a 'state of melancholy madness' by its enforced imprisonment and activity. There is, then, something inherently wrong or evil about the society of Coketown and this is stressed further by the description of the 'interminable serpents of smoke' from the 'tall chimneys'. The serpent is perhaps reminiscent of the serpent in the Garden of Eden which corrupted mankind, and so once again the imagery serves to suggest the evil of the society being described. Indeed, the very way in which Coketown is described provides a comment on the principles of mass-production, mechanisation and money upon which the town is founded. Coketown, and the principles upon which it is founded, is both enslaving, and evil.

(c) *Try to say how the passage relates to the novel as a whole.* I now need to pull back and relate these impressions to my ideas about the novel as a whole. I have already mentioned the idea that the characters who believe in facts try to impose *their* view of the world upon the other characters. They can do this because they possess money, and money provides them with the power to impose their beliefs on other people. The passage above reinforces this point by showing that this power affects every part of people's lives. It could be argued that *Hard Times* is about the way in which the people with money and power force the people without money and without power to live in an unnatural, squalid and mechanised world.

(d) *Search for anything distinctive in the passage, particularly in the area of style, which you have not already noted.* What is particularly interesting about this passage in terms of style is the way in which the mechanised world is reflected in the actual style of writing. The final, long sentence, for example, seems to create the very mechanical ethos of Coketown, piling up similar phrases: 'It contained several large streets all very like one another, and many small streets still more like one another.' The repetition here is paralleled throughout the passage by the repetition of particular words which further support the effect of a mechanical world: all the people are 'equally like one another', they work 'the same hours', make the 'same sound upon the same pavements', and every day of their lives was 'the same as yesterday'. The sameness of mechanisation and mass-production upon which Coketown is founded is reflected not only in the lives of its inhabitants, but also in the repetition of the phrases and words Dickens uses to describe it.

4   *Select a third passage for discussion*

I hope you can see just how simple this method of analysis is: all that it involves is having a few controlling ideas and then interpreting passages in the light of these ideas. It is a simple method, but it should enable you to produce your own distinctive reading of the novel as you respond to what you think is central in a passage and then relate it to your developing sense of the work as a whole. One of my controlling ideas is the notion that the imposition of Gradgrind's and Bounderby's belief in practical necessity not only affects the external, physical world, but also poisons and corrupts the internal, spiritual world of the individual. It is an idea which is seen most clearly in Dickens's presentation of Bitzer, the model pupil of the Bounderby–Gradgrind system. In this passage Bitzer has apprehended Tom in Sleary's circus, just as Thomas Gradgrind is attempting to help his son flee the country:

They went back into the booth, Sleary shutting the door to keep intruders out. Bitzer, still holding the paralysed culprit by the collar, stood in the ring, blinking at his old patron through the darkness of the twilight.

'Bitzer,' said Mr Gradgrind, broken down, and miserably submissive to him, 'have you a heart?'

'The circulation, sir,' returned Bitzer, smiling at the oddity of the question, 'couldn't be carried on without one. No man, sir, acquainted with the facts established by Harvey, relating to the circulation of the blood, can doubt that I have a heart.'

'Is it accessible,' cried Mr Gradgrind, 'to any compassionate influence?'

'It is accessible to reason, sir,' returned the excellent young man. 'And to nothing else.'

They stood looking at each other; Mr Gradgrind's face as white as the pursuer's. (pp. 302–3)

(a) *Search for an opposition or tension within the passage.* The tension here is neatly focused on the conflict between Thomas Gradgrind, one of the *exponents* of the Gradgrind–Bounderby system and the belief in practical necessity, and Bitzer and young Tom, two of the *products* of the Gradgrind–Bounderby system. The passage itself occurs after Louisa has left Bounderby and has turned to her father for emotional support, and illustrates the extent to which Thomas Gradgrind's belief in practical necessity has broken down under the strain placed upon it by his natural affection for his children, Tom and Louisa. What we can say, then, is that the passage reflects the same conflict as we identified at the beginning of this book: the conflict between money and self-interest (the world of facts), and the world of natural love and affection.

(b) *Analyse the details of the passage, relating them to the opposition already noted.* The details of the text illustrate the last point precisely. Bitzer, in the opening scene of the novel, is the boy who identifies a cow as a 'Quadruped. Graminivorous' (p. 50). Confronted here by the world of the emotions, he is incapable of responding: 'Have you a heart?' asks Thomas Gradgrind, and Bitzer can only smile 'at the oddity of the question'. Of course he has a heart, because the Gradgrind–Bounderby system has taught him that he has a heart. It is a fact, but nothing else. Bitzer has no feelings, no compassion for his fellow human beings; he is open only to reason. Gradgrind, thus confronted by the harshness of his system in the face of natural affection, is 'broken down'.

(c) *Try to say how the passage relates to the novel as a whole.* The force of this passage is that it makes clear the foolishness of the Gradgrind–Bounderby system as we see Gradgrind forced to become the compassionate father he naturally is. What makes the scene more poignant still is that both Tom and Bitzer are products of his own system, yet both are human failures; Tom is a criminal, and Bitzer an inhuman and unthinking automaton. This is consistent with the conflict in the novel as a whole between the world of money and power and the world of love and natural affection, and illustrates the effect of the Gradgrind–Bounderby system not only on the external world, but also on the internal, spiritual and emotional life of the individual.

(d) *Search for anything distinctive about the passage, particularly in the area of style, which you have already noted.* Dickens sets the scene in the enclosed world of Sleary's circus ('Sleary shutting the door to keep intruders out'), a world incomprehensible to the world of facts. Consequently, Bitzer quite literally cannot *see,* because he cannot *understand;* he is standing in the ring, 'blinking at his patron in the darkness of the twilight'. Similarly, Bitzer and Gradgrind are left at the end of the scene 'looking at each other', but each incapable of understanding the other. This lack of understanding reinforces what the dialogue suggests: not only are the two worlds of money and love in conflict with each other, but they are also incomprehensible to each other. Bitzer is quite incapable of grasping the meaning of Gradgrind's question, and replies in the only way he knows – factually.

5   *Select a fourth passage for discussion*

My analysis of the novel so far has centred on the conflict between the world of money and the world of love, and has suggested that the world of money actively poisons and corrupts not just the external world in which the characters live, but also the internal, spiritual world. I now want to look at how Sissy Jupe fits into this scheme of things. I have selected a passage where Sissy confronts Harthouse and tells him that he will never see Louisa again:

> Mr Harthouse drew a long breath; and, if ever man found himself in the position of not knowing what to say, made the discovery beyond all question that he was so circumstanced. The childlike ingenuousness with which his visitor spoke, her modest fearlessness, her truthfulness which put all artifice

aside, her entire forgetfulness of herself in her earnest quiet holding to the object with which she had come; all this, together with her reliance on his easily-given promise – which in itself shamed him – presented something in which he was so inexperienced, and against which he knew any of his usual weapons would fall so powerless, that not a word could he rally to his relief.
(pp. 252–3)

(a) *Search for an opposition or tension within the passage.* The conflict or tension here is that between the worldly-wise James Harthouse and the innocent Sissy Jupe. What is particularly interesting is that Harthouse is defeated by Sissy's complete innocence.

(b) *Analyse the details of the passage, relating them to the opposition already noted.* The worldly-wise Harthouse, Louisa's seducer, and political intriguer, is defenceless when faced with pure and simple truth – Sissy's 'modest fearlessness, her truthfulness which put all artifice aside ... against which he knew any of his usual weapons would fall so powerless, that not a word could he rally to his relief'. Harthouse, normally so adept in the ways of the world, in flattery and the well-turned phrase, is unable to defend himself against the simple truth Sissy represents.

(c) *Try to say how the passage relates to the novel as a whole.* The passage reflects the way Dickens presents the childlike simplicity of spirit of certain characters throughout the novel. But of these Sissy is the only one to escape the Gradgrind–Bounderby system altogether, just as Bitzer is the only one to be wholly indoctrinated by it. This gives to the potentially gloomy vision that Dickens presents in *Hard Times* a distinct sense of optimism: if truth and a simplicity of spirit are to be maintained in the face of relentless indoctrination by political systems, economic systems, or whatever, it is in characters like Sissy Jupe that Dickens puts his trust.

(d) *Search for anything distinctive in the passage, particularly in the area of style, which you have not already noted.* In terms of style, this passage is interesting because by cataloguing all of Sissy's *attributes* ('her childlike ingenuousness ... her truthfulness which put all artifice aside ... her entire forgetfulness of herself ...'), it also catalogues, by *not* stating them, all of Harthouse's *failings*: his sophisticated affectation, his greed and deceit, his excessive self-interest. The point is further emphasised by the use of one word in particular, the word 'inexperienced'. This word is often used to indicate an unsophisticated approach to life – Sissy, for example, could be said to be 'inexperienced' in the ways of the world. But in this passage it is used to refer to Harthouse, for Harthouse, although fully experienced in the ways of the *world*, is wholly 'inexperienced' in *truth*. In short, what we have here is the basic conflict between money, greed, affectation and self-interest, and a natural simplicity of spirit. Sissy's simple 'childlike ingenuousness' wins through against all the odds, and, as the end of the novel tells us, she is the only one to find complete happiness in her later life.

6   *Have I achieved a sufficiently complex sense of the novel?*

By this stage, having looked at four passages, you should have pieced together a view of the novel. If you are still puzzled, look at more passages until you feel you have worked out a coherent reading. Your ideas might well develop in a very different direction from mine, but this is the whole point about this method of looking at a text – that it allows you, as you move from passage to passage, systematically to develop your own interpretation of a novel. At this stage, however, stop and ask yourself whether you feel you have got to grips with the work. Try to be precise: what still puzzles you about the novel?

One big gap that I am aware of in my analysis so far of *Hard Times* is that, since I have concentrated on the major characters and events, I have said very little about the sub-plot of Stephen Blackpool and his friend Rachael. The sensible thing to do now, therefore, is to look at a passage involving these characters. There are really two choices here. The first could be a passage from early in the novel when Blackpool's wife returns and she is cared for by Rachael. The interesting thing about this passage is that Blackpool very nearly allows his wife to poison herself, until she is stopped by Rachael. But the second choice may be a better one for analysis. This concerns the time when Blackpool is discovered by Rachael and Louisa. He has just been dragged out of the disused mineshaft into which he had fallen, and is near to death:

'Thou'rt in great pain, my own dear Stephen?'
    'I ha' been, but not now. I ha' been – dreadful, and dree, and long, my dear – but 'tis ower now. Ah, Rachael, aw a muddle! Fro' first to last, a muddle!' The spectre of his old look seemed to pass as he said the word.
    'I ha' fell into th' pit, my dear, as have cost wi'in the knowledge o' old fok

now living, hundred and hundreds o' men's lives – fathers, sons, brothers, dear to thousands an' thousands, an' keepin' 'em fro' want and hunger. I ha' fell into a pit that ha' been, wi' the' fire-damp, crueller than battle. I ha' read on't in the public petition, as onny one may read, fro' the men that works in pits, in which they ha' pray'n an pray'n the lawmakers for Christ's sake not to let their work be murder to 'em, but to spare 'em for the' wives and children that they loves as well as gentlefok loves theirs. When it were in work, it killed wi'out need; when 'tis let alone, it kills wi'out need. See how we die an' no need, one way an' another – in a muddle – every day!'

He faintly said it, without any anger against any one. Merely as the truth. (pp. 289–90)

I must admit that as a student I would probably have found it very difficult to know what to say about a passage such as this, mainly because I then had no real idea of how to approach a text. But any passage can be coped with if you approach it in a systematic way. Part of the secret is telling yourself that the passage must be dealing with issues which you have already registered as central to the novel.

(a) *Search for an opposition or tension within the passage.* You might find it hard to spot an opposition here, but bear in mind the idea we have already developed that the world of money actively poisons and corrupts not just the external world in which the characters live, but also the internal, spiritual world. What strikes me in this passage is that there is a contrast between the threatening presence of the pit, which has killed thousands of people, and Blackpool's simple desire that we should all be able to live happily together.

(b) *Analyse the details of the passage, relating them to the opposition already noted.* The words chosen emphasise the contrast effectively: the pit is described as 'crueller than battle'; when it was a working pit it 'killed wi'out need', and now it is disused it still 'kills wi'out need'. On the other hand, the work the pit has provided has kept generations of people free from 'want and hunger'. To be free from 'want and hunger' is a natural desire of all people, as natural as the bond and affection between people of all classes: the poor, labouring classes love their wives and children just 'as well as gentlefok loves theirs'. So the opposition here is between the murderous nature of the pit, and the simple desire Blackpool feels for people to love one another.

(c) *Try to say how the passage relates to the novel as a whole.* The passage emphasises the extent of the control of the world of money over the lives of ordinary people. The pit is ugly, dangerous and unnatural. It has been put in an otherwise beautiful and natural countryside apparently for no other purpose than to make money and kill people. Consequently, the pit becomes a symbol for the ugly, corrupting world of money which destroys the natural beauty of the world and the natural affection between people. But, despite all this, the natural world beyond the pit retains its beauty, just as Blackpool retains his natural integrity of spirit and his simple desire that we should all be free to care for and love one another. This reinforces our earlier perception that the world of money is capable of poisoning and corrupting the internal, spiritual world of *some* people, but that others – such as Sissy Jupe and Stephen Blackpool – even though they may be physically killed by the world of money, remain emotionally pure of its effects because of their natural simplicity of spirit.

What makes all this particularly interesting is that, if we now recall the earlier scene in which Blackpool is tempted into letting his wife poison herself, we can see some interesting parallels. Blackpool nearly allows his wife to poison herself not because he has never loved her but because the world of money has destroyed 'the woman he had married eighteen years before' (p. 124). For Blackpool to be a participant in his wife's death would make him her murderer, but he is saved by Rachael, who wakes just in time to stop his wife drinking the poison. Consequently, Blackpool's immortal soul is rescued from the pit of hell by Rachael: 'Thou'rt an angel; it may be, thou hast saved my soul alive!' he tells her (p. 125). It is ironic that when he is rescued from the Old Hell Shaft, the disused mine-pit into which he has fallen, he realises the simple truth of human existence in a world dominated by money: 'See how we die an' no need, one way an' another – in a muddle – every day!' he says, 'Merely as the truth.'

(d) *Search for anything distinctive about the passage, particularly in the area of style, which you have not already noted.* We can see this concern mirrored in the style of the passage also. When Dickens is describing the world of Coketown and Gradgrind's and Bounderby's world of facts, the sentences are balanced, precise, regular. Even the people speak in well-balanced and planned sentences, working their way through their points with remorseless logic. But in this piece Blackpool speaks in dialect. Sentences are often unfinished, grammatically deviant, and contain odd words and pronunciation. This, of course, is an affront to the regular, ordered world represented by Coketown and Gradgrind and Bounderby. Even more ironic is Blackpool's recognition that the world of fact is also a world of 'muddle'. Organisation can apply only to things which are capable of being organised: natural love and affection, like Blackpool's final recognition of the truth, defy the order and organisation represented by Coketown, Gradgrind and Bounderby. Consequently, Blackpool's speech is disordered and disorganised, like the love and truth about which he speaks: love is untidy, but it is also a redeeming feature of humanity.

Having looked at this passage in some detail I feel I can now sum up the impression that the novel as a whole makes on me. Different readers will interpret the evidence differently, but it seems to me that Dickens is writing about the corrupting effect of the world of money both on the natural world and on the natural affection that there is between individuals. This is a potentially gloomy vision, since we live in a world in which the economic social order is of great importance: power still resides in money, and people are still judged by how much money they have or don't have. But Dickens suggests also that there is hope, that natural love and affection is still to be found in certain people – such as Sleary, Sissy Jupe and Stephen Blackpool – and even if this natural love and affection is destroyed in others – such as Bitzer, Harthouse, Gradgrind and Bounderby. At the end of the novel, it is Sissy Jupe who wins through, while Bounderby dies of a fit in Coketown High Street.

There is nothing particularly original about this reading of the novel, but criticism does not need to strain after wildly original interpretations. Your criticism of a novel has to be imaginative, you have to respond to the text's ideas, but what really matters is that, as in this analysis of *Hard Times*, you work closely from the evidence of the text to build a coherent reading of the novel which does honestly reflect your own response to the novel.

II Aspects of the novel

The first part of this chapter has shown you how to respond critically to particular scenes, characters and details in a text, but I now want to go on to consider the idea that Dickens's novels are comic novels. This is an aspect of Dickens's work which often features in examination questions, and it will be useful to look here at how the comic functions in *Hard Times*, since similar comic features will be encountered in all of Dickens's novels.

In many ways, *Hard Times* may not seem to be a particularly comic novel: the story of a young girl deserted by her father, of a daughter who prostitutes her emotions for her father's wrongheaded principles, of a son who becomes a criminal and causes the death of an innocent man is not on the surface a funny story. For all this, *Hard Times* is still a comic novel, because in it people are seen as types or caricatures illustrating particular human weaknesses – such as greed or self-interest – and this allows these weaknesses to be exaggerated to comic proportions. Comedy in Dickens's novels in part consists of laughing at these absurd, pompous characters trapped in situations in which they are bound to reveal their own pomposity, affectation and self-interest. But be careful here. The obvious response is to say that such characters *deserve* to be trapped in these situations, but you do need to go beyond this and consider how the comic exposition of a certain character fits into the larger scheme of things. The discovery by the interfering and obnoxious Mrs Sparsit of Bounderby's mother is a case in point:

> 'Sir,' explained that worthy woman, 'I trust it is my good fortune to produce a person you have much desired to find. Stimulated by my wish to relieve your mind, sir, and connecting together such imperfect clues to the part of the country in which that person might be supposed to reside, as have been afforded by the young woman Rachael, fortunately now present to identify, I have had the happiness to succeed, and to bring that person with me – I need not say most unwillingly on her part. It has not been, sir, without some trouble that I have effected this; but trouble in your service is to me a pleasure, and hunger, thirst, and cold, a real gratification.'
>
> Here Mrs Sparsit ceased; for Mr Bounderby's visage exhibited an extraordinary combination of all possible colours and expressions of discomfiture, as old Mrs Pegler was disclosed to his view.
>
> 'Why, what do you mean by this?' was his highly unexpected demand, in great warmth. 'I ask you, what do you mean by this, Mrs Sparsit, ma'am?'
>
> 'Sir!' exclaimed Mrs Sparsit faintly.
>
> 'Why don't you mind your own business, ma'am?' roared Bounderby. 'How dare you go and poke your officious nose into my family affairs?' (pp. 278–9)

(a) *Search for an opposition or tension within the passage.* There is a conflict here between Mrs Sparsit's triumphant tone and the angry way in which Bounderby reacts. Mrs Sparsit delivers old Mrs Pegler up to Bounderby believing that she has caught the bank robber. What she doesn't know, but what the reader by now does know, is that old Mrs Pegler is none other than Bounderby's mother. What the passage thus emphasises is both Mrs Sparsit's intolerable interfering and Bounderby's self-glorifying misrepresentation of his past, and in so doing it shows how these characters are trapped by their own weaknesses: if it were not for Mrs Sparsit's interfering nature and for Bounderby's self-deceit, this ironic confrontation could never happen.

(b) *Analyse the details of the passage, relating them to the opposition already noted.* There are two aspects of Mrs Sparsit's character revealed in the details of the text: first, her interfering nature, by which she forces old Mrs Pegler 'most unwillingly on her part' to Bounderby's home; and, secondly, her obsequiousness, in which 'trouble in your service is a pleasure, and hunger, thirst, and cold, a real gratification'. Bounderby, because of his vanity and snobbery, normally responds favourably to Mrs Sparsit's fawning, but here he 'roars' at her, 'How dare you go and poke your officious nose into my family affairs?' What is interesting is Bounderby's reference to Mrs Sparsit's 'officious nose', since it is Mrs Sparsit's 'Coriolanian nose' (p. 84) which he has earlier seen as symbolic of her 'ancient stock' (p. 83). Bounderby, for once shocked out of his self-glorification, sees her nose for what it really is: not 'Coriolanian' and symbolic of her refined breeding, but 'officious'.

(c) *Try to say how the passage relates to the novel as a whole.* Setting this piece in the wider context of the whole novel, we can perceive also a fairly obvious tension between love and money. It is after all quite natural that a mother should want to see her son, and that a son should display love and affection for his mother. But Bounderby cannot do this. His obsession with himself and with the world of money has so poisoned his inner, spiritual nature that he has pensioned his mother off and denied her. He has, in fact, gone further than this, by claiming earlier that his mother deserted him when he was a child and left him to the brutality of a drunken grandmother. This behaviour is wholly unnatural, and is opposed by Mrs Pegler's timid, natural desire to see her son and to be proud of his success. The point to appreciate here is that even in comic scenes such as the above, we can still perceive the broader thematic concerns that we have already detected in the novel as a whole.

(d) *Search for anything distinctive about the passage, particularly in the area of style, which you have not already noted.* The interplay of comedy and the novel's broader concerns is subtly reinforced by light stylistic touches. Dickens puts into the mouth of Mrs Sparsit speeches which are capable of being interpreted in two ways. Take, for example, the following: 'I trust it is my good fortune to produce a person you have much desired to find.' This – like the sentence which follows it – is ambiguous in the situation in which it occurs. First, the reader can interpret this to mean that Mrs Sparsit has discovered Bounderby's long-lost mother, and it is *natural* that he should want to see her again, and *natural* that Mrs Sparsit should want to go out of her way to 'relieve' Bounderby's mind, since it is *natural* that he would be concerned about her safety. But secondly, Mrs Sparsit's intentions are in fact spiteful, interfering, obsequious and *unnatural;* the only reason she has dragged Mrs Pegler to Bounderby's home is that she has found another innocent person (in lieu of Stephen Blackpool) to charge with the bank robbery. And the only reason she has done this is because of her own self-interest, thinking her actions will increase Bounderby's respect for her. In fact, the result is quite the opposite, since she has inadvertently discovered his mother, and not the bank-robber. So we can notice how even in small stylistic details the passage reflects the constant opposition in *Hard Times* between the natural love and simplicity of spirit illustrated by Mrs Pegler, and the unnatural affectation and self-interest illustrated by Mrs Sparsit and Bounderby.

I hope you can see from the above that the way in which the comic functions in Dickens's novels is quite complicated. But don't be put off by this: each additional scene you look at will not only help you to clarify in your own mind how the comic works but also will provide a fresh slant and add to the overall complexity of your analysis. When you work on other scenes, ask yourself, as I did with this passage, how the idea of natural love is reflected and how the world of money is reflected in the extract. Most of the characters are, like Mrs Pegler, capable of exhibiting a natural love for each other but are unable to do so because of the way in which the world of money imposes upon them. Others, such as Mrs Sparsit and Bounderby, are wholly incapable of exhibiting any natural affection because they are too much a part of the world of money, self-interest and affectation.

A whole group of characters in *Hard Times,* Sleary's circus people, can be looked at in a similar way. It is not enough to say that the circus folk are mildly amusing and provide some light relief; they too must reflect the broader concerns of the novel, and it is again the case that the best way to crystallise your sense of this is to look closely at a passage, or passages, in which they appear. In the following extract, Bounderby and Gradgrind have gone in search of Sissy Jupe's father at Sleary's circus, and receive a fairly hostile reception:

> 'Kidderminster,' said Mr Childers, raising his voice, 'stow that! – Sir,' to Mr Gradgrind, 'I was addressing myself to you. You may or may not be aware (for perhaps you have not been much in the audience), that Jupe has missed his tip very often, lately.'
>
> 'Has – what has he missed?' asked Mr Gradgrind, glancing at the potent Bounderby for assistance.
>
> 'Missed his tip.'
>
> 'Offered at the garters four times last night, and never done 'em once,' said Master Kidderminster. 'Missed his tip at the banners, too, and was loose in his ponging.'
>
> 'Didn't do what he ought to do. Was short in his leaps and bad in his tumbling,' Mr Childers interpreted.
>
> 'Oh!' said Mr Gradgrind, 'that is tip, is it?'
>
> 'In a general way that's missing his tip,' Mr E W B Childers answered.
>
> 'Nine oils, Merrylegs, missing tips, garters, banners, and ponging, eh!' ejaculated Bounderby, with his laugh of laughs. 'Queer sort of company, too, for a man who has raised himself.'   (p. 73)

This passage draws a straightforward contrast between Gradgrind and Bounderby and the world of the circus folk, and this is most noticeable in that Gradgrind and Bounderby are unable to understand what it is the circus folk are talking about. The passage is likely to strike you primarily as funny, and it might seem very hard to see how it could possibly have any broader significance in the text as a whole. But think of the division within society represented by the world of Coketown and the world of Sleary's circus, and how this is symbolic of the division between money and love. It is interesting to note that, even when the circus folk attempt to explain what they mean to Gradgrind and Bounderby, Bounderby is capable only of relating the oddity of the circus world back to himself and his own affected stance in the world: 'Queer sort of company, too, for a man who has raised himself.' Here he refers to

himself – he is the man who has 'raised himself' – but there is no
consideration of just what it means for Jupe to 'have missed his
tip'. On the other hand, it is clear that Jupe's missing his tip is a
matter of communal interest to the circus folk, and Childers
assumes that it will be a matter of some concern to Gradgrind and
Bounderby also: 'You may or may not be aware (for perhaps you
have not been much in the audience) that Jupe has missed his tip
very often, lately', he says. The assumption Childers is making
here is that, had Gradgrind and Bounderby been in the audience,
they would *of course* have noticed that Jupe had missed his tip,
and would therefore be concerned about it, just as the circus folk
are. Gradgrind and Bounderby cannot be concerned about it
because, first, they don't know what it is, and secondly, they don't
know how to be concerned about another person anyway.

Finally, it is worth noting that this passage, like the passage in
which Blackpool dies, makes use of a number of highly deviant
words and grammatical constructions. This again represents just
how wide the gulf is between Gradgrind's and Bounderby's world
of facts and money, and Sleary's circus world of simplicity of spirit
and natural affection. They simply speak quite different lan-
guages; since Gradgrind and Bounderby do not share in the
emotions of the circus world, they cannot share in its language,
either. Although the passage is funny, then, it is in fact making a
very serious point about the darker, irrational desires which
motivate humans – such as Bounderby's obsession with himself –
and which are a part of the world of money. Consequently, the
social façade which the world of money constructs around itself is
seen to be a paper-thin covering over basically selfish desires:
desires such as greed, lust, self-interest and affectation. Such a
view of the world is ultimately a disturbing one, since we live in a
world which bears more similarities to the world of money than it
bears to Sleary's circus world.

The effect of *Hard Times*, therefore, may be to encourage the
reader to look more critically at his or her own society, since the
novel is presenting that society as little more than an elaborate
charade, founded on the most questionable moral and economic
principles. An interesting thing to notice about this is that the
novel achieves this effect by telling a story. Not only does it tell a
story, but it peoples its story with characters who, in the strict
sense, are nothing like real people in the real world. The comic
characters in Dickens's novels are not 'real' characters even in the

sense that characters in a novel can be real. They are instead, massive caricatures or types who allow normally hidden, basic human desires and failings to be exaggerated to comic proportions and made fun of. Always remember, however, that there is a serious side to all this, since we see, in this disruptive view of the world, some of the essential characteristics and failings of our own society.

What should be obvious by now is how far we have developed our analysis from the beginning of this chapter, in which I merely noted a simple opposition in the novel. But my whole analysis has developed from that simple opposition, allowing us to see the way in which Dickens's actual writing reflects a more complex set of values in conflict. The major point is that wherever you turn in a Dickens novel you will encounter some sense of a conflict between money and love and a whole range of other, related tensions. Whether you look at scenes, characters or specific details in the text you will find the same conflict being reiterated time and again, echoing at each turn in the story the novel's larger concerns. You might have to niggle away at some details and situations for some time before you can work out their place in the scheme of things, but eventually you should always be able to see how they help create the broader impression the novel offers of the potentially poisoning and corrupting effect of the world of money and political and economic systems upon the natural love and affection we have for our fellow humans.

3

Great Expectations

I Constructing an overall analysis

Great Expectations belongs to the type of novel known as a *Bildungsroman,* or education novel. The phrase I shall use to describe it is 'education novel', but I mention the German term *Bildungsroman* (which means the same thing) because you may well encounter it if you read other critical works about *Great Expectations.* Broadly speaking, the education novel tells the story of the personal and moral development of its central character. By the end of the novel this central character has learnt something about the world or about himself or herself, and has become a very different person from the one we first met in the novel's opening.

In *Great Expectations* the central character is Pip, and he tells his story from the point of view of his adulthood, looking back over the events which have formed his character. All this has certain implications for the form of the novel: because Pip tells his own story directly to the reader, we have the impression of being able to see into his mind as he speaks. In addition, this use of first-person narration seems to create a much stronger sense of reality than in the previous novel we looked at, *Hard Times*; but it creates other effects too, and we shall look at some of these later. But the first thing to do is to organise your response to the text itself, as this will enable you to build your own view of the novel. The place to start, as always, is with some thoughts about the novel's plot.

1   *After reading the novel, think about the story and what kind of pattern you can see in the plot*

Great Expectations tells the story of Philip Pirrip, known as 'Pip', an orphan brought up by his bad-tempered sister and her warm-hearted husband, Joe Gargery, the village blacksmith.

As a child, Pip is confronted by an escaped convict on the marshes, and the convict – Abel Magwitch – forces Pip to bring him food and a file. Magwitch is recaptured, however, after a struggle with another escaped convict, Compeyson, and both are returned to their prison ship. Some time later Pip is sent for by Miss Havisham, who, having been jilted on her wedding-day many years previously, has lived cut off from society in her home, Satis House, ever since. Miss Havisham has an adopted daughter, the beautiful Estella, whom she has brought up as a cold, heartless child to wreak her revenge on men. Pip falls in love with Estella but she immediately rebuffs him, and as a result he begins to despise his lowly origins. When Pip is fourteen, Miss Havisham pays for him to be apprenticed to Joe Gargery, the village blacksmith, and his visits to Satis House and to Estella come to an end.

Four years into his apprenticeship Pip receives a visit from an Old Bailey lawyer, Jaggers, whom he had met at Satis House some years previously. Jaggers has been sent to tell him that he has ready money to make Pip a gentleman, and expectations of great wealth for him. The money comes from an unknown benefactor, and the only condition attached to it is that Pip must never attempt to discover the identity of this unknown benefactor. Pip immediately assumes his benefactor to be Miss Havisham, and assumes also that she is preparing him to be a gentleman so that he may in time marry Estella. He goes to London to learn to be a gentleman. There he becomes friends with Herbert Pocket, a nephew of Miss Havisham's, whom he had previously met at Satis House.

In London, Pip becomes proud and snobbish and neglects his old friends, but particularly the loving blacksmith, Joe Gargery. He gradually gets himself further and further into debt, and is continually snubbed by Estella, who is now also living in London. It is at this point that Pip's real benefactor is revealed. This turns out to be Abel Magwitch, the convict he helped on the marshes when he was a child, and who has in the meantime made a fortune as a transported convict in Australia. Pip at first rejects the lowly Magwitch, and is ashamed that the source of his present wealth comes from a criminal. Pip learns that Estella has married the boorish Bentley Drummle, and this throws him further into the depths of depression.

Magwitch is finally recaptured when he is betrayed by his old enemy Compeyson, and is sentenced to death. But he dies before he can be executed. Pip is left penniless, although he has discovered that Magwitch is Estella's father, that her real mother is Jaggers's housekeeper, and that Compeyson is the lover who jilted Miss Havisham on her wedding-day. After a long illness in which he is nursed patiently by Joe, who also pays off his debts, Pip sees the idle foolishness of his previous way of life and returns to his home village, intent on asking Biddy, a childhood friend, to marry him.

But on his return to the blacksmith's home he discovers Biddy and Joe on their wedding-day, and determines to put his own life in order by going to work as a clerk for the company in which Herbert is now a partner. Eleven years later he visits the ruins of Satis House (Miss Havisham is now dead), where he meets Estella. Mistreated by Drummle, Estella is now a widow and a reformed, affectionate woman. Their hands clasp, with the promise of love, happiness and marriage in the inevitable future – at least in one version of the novel's ending.

As we have seen in previous chapters, the way to start making sense of a novel is to look for some type of pattern in the plot. This pattern can take many forms, but a good rule of thumb is to look for a situation, or a particular type of character, or a particular relationship between characters being repeated several times. Remember, though, that in a Dickens novel the overall pattern we can expect to find will eventually focus upon a conflict or tension between money and love. This applies even where, as here, we have a fairly long and intricate plot. This in itself, however, can tell us a great deal about the novel.

One of the reasons why the plot is so complicated is that it is being reported by the first-person narrator, Pip, and Pip – unlike an omniscient narrator – cannot know everything about all the characters and all their relationships. The result of this is that things are gradually discovered, both by the reader and by Pip. What gradually comes out in Pip's story is that many of the characters are either unwittingly related to each other (Magwitch, for instance, being Estella's father) or want to keep their relationships secret. When Pip is in London, for example, posing as a gentleman, he wants to keep his relationship with Joe Gargery a secret from his new friends, the Finches of the Grove. Similarly, Herbert Pocket has to keep his relationship with Clara a secret because he knows his snobbish mother will not approve of her. What we have to ask ourselves is how all these secret relationships illustrate something about the conflict between love and money.

We can begin by thinking about the concept of a relationship between people. Normally, this has to do with family ties, or sexual and emotional ties between people. One of its identifying characteristics is that it has to do with feelings, with love for another person. Why then, should so many of the relationships in *Great Expectations* have to be kept a secret? The simple answer is: money.

Think, for example, of the various secret benefactors in the novel. Pip believes that Miss Havisham is his secret benefactor, when in fact it is Magwitch – but Pip can ask no questions, since it must be kept a secret. Later Pip arranges, with Miss Havisham as a secret benefactor, to establish Herbert in business – but the whole thing must be kept a secret. One of the reasons for wanting to be a benefactor is presumably a desire to help somebody by giving them money. But in all the cases in the novel – with the notable exception of Joe, who openly pays off Pip's debts – to give financial help to somebody means hiding who you are, and hiding your relationship to that person. In other words, the thing which intervenes between characters in most of the relationships in the novel is money. Money actually obscures the expression of love, and this is a major theme in the novel. What is particularly interesting, however, is that all the characters have the need for love and for a relationship with another person, but this is consistently obscured by financial considerations.

In such a situation characters become utilities: Estella is handed over to Miss Havisham by Jaggers to save her mother from the gallows; Pip is bought off by Miss Havisham when she has finished toying with his emotions, and made Joe's apprentice; even Compeyson's jilting of Miss Havisham was motivated by money. Looked at in this way, the whole novel can be seen to stem from a basic conflict between love and money, and it is this conflict which occupies Pip in his narrative. When he goes to London he leaves Joe's natural love and simplicity of spirit behind him. But in London, and although he has ready money in his pocket, his snobbishness forces him to keep his relationship with Joe a secret; he is snubbed by Estella, disdained by the Finches, and ultimately without love because he is emotionally alone. What this suggests is that all people, no matter what material wealth they possess, need the love and friendship of other people, but that money can make that love and friendship impossible to have.

2   *Analyse the opening paragraph or two of the novel and try to build on the ideas you have established so far*

Once you have identified the conflict which is at the centre of *Great Expectations*, the next stage is to look at the opening of the novel itself, since it is here that Dickens's unique handling of the topic is going to be most apparent. This is how the novel starts (page references relate to the Penguin edition, 1976):

> My father's family name being Pirrip, and my christian name Philip, my infant tongue could make of both names nothing longer or more explicit than Pip. So, I called myself Pip, and came to be called Pip.
>
> I give Pirrip as my father's family name, on the authority of his tombstone and my sister – Mrs Joe Gargery, who married the blacksmith. As I never saw my father or my mother, and never saw any likeness of either of them (for their days were long before the days of photographs), my fancies regarding what they were like, were unreasonably derived from their tombstones.
>
> (p. 35)

The first thing to do with this passage is, as always, to find some form of opposition or tension within it. The passage itself is straightforward enough: it introduces the novel's central character, Pip. But if you think about the way in which it does that, you will immediately notice that there is a tension of some kind between Pip the child and the family of which he should be a part. That is, this child can report who he is only on the basis of fragmentary evidence gleaned from inanimate or distant sources: 'I give Pirrip as my father's family name, on the authority of his tombstone.' He has no father to tell him anything, no mother, not even an image of them, 'for their days were long before the days of photographs'. Even his one surviving relative – his sister – is in a sense no relative to him at all, since even she does not share his name: 'and my sister – Mrs Joe Gargery'.

You might be tempted to argue that all the passage tells us is that Pip is an orphan. But this would be to miss all the details of the text, and to miss how the passage relates to the novel as a whole. If we now extend the idea that here we have a child curiously isolated from the family of which he should be a part, we should begin to see how the passage focuses on the novel's central themes.

For example, not only is this child wholly alone in the world, but he literally does not know who he is. Since he has no family he has no relation to anything at all. Consequently, he is forced into the situation of having to provide himself with a name: 'I called myself Pip, and came to be called Pip'. A child's name is normally provided by the parents, and that assumes a child's relationship with the past and a personal, family history to support it. But Pip has no past, and hence no relationship to anything. Consequently, not only does he possess nothing (and much of *Great Expectations* is about the desire to possess), but he also has no status in the world, because he is wholly alienated from it. He has no place anywhere, and is nobody. We could safely project from this that much of the novel will have to do with Pip trying to become somebody, trying to discover who he is. The only way in which he can do this, as the above passage suggests, is by building relationships with other people, since he has none to start with. The effect of the passage as a whole, then, is that it impresses very forcefully on our minds a sense of Pip's isolation in the world, and the need for him to build relationships with other people in order to discover who he is. The novel details his successes and failures in this quest to discover a person in himself and a position in the world.

3   *Select a second passage for discussion*

The only loving relationship in which we see Pip in the early part of the novel is with Joe Gargery, his sister's husband. Any passage in which he and Pip appear together will tell you a lot about the closeness of their simple relationship, but it may be more productive to look at Pip and Joe together being confronted by another character who is not a part of their relationship. The extract I have chosen describes Joe and Pip at Satis House, where they have been summoned by Miss Havisham, who plans to pay for Pip to be apprenticed to Joe:

'Have you brought his indentures with you?' asked Miss Havisham.
'Well, Pip, you know, replied Joe, as if that were a little unreasonable, 'you yourself see me put 'em in my 'at, and therefore you know as they are here.' With which he took them out, and gave them, not to Miss Havisham, but to me. I am afraid I was ashamed of the dear good fellow – I *know* I was ashamed of him – when I saw that Estella stood at the back of Miss Havisham's chair, and that her eyes laughed mischievously. I took the indentures out of his hand and gave them to Miss Havisham.
'You expected,' said Miss Havisham, as she looked them over, 'no premium with the boy?'
'Joe!' I remonstrated; for he made no reply at all.

'Why don't you answer—'

'Pip,' returned Joe, cutting me short as if he were hurt, 'which I meantersay that were not a question requiring a answer betwixt yourself and me, and which you know the answer to be full well No. You know it to be No, Pip, and wherefore should I say it?'

Miss Havisham glanced at him as if she understood what he really was, better than I had thought possible, seeing what he was there; and took up a little bag from the table beside her.

'Pip has earned a premium here,' she said, 'and here it is. There are five-and-twenty guineas in this bag. Give it to your master, Pip.' (p. 129)

Before I start on the analysis of this passage, I want to remind you that I am mainly concerned in this book with illustrating a method of analysing a novel. An important part of this method has to do with noticing the novelist's use of particular techniques or patterns, so don't forget that techniques or patterns you notice in one novel will probably recur in other novels, and will function in much the same way. This can give you a starting-point for your analysis of other, apparently quite dissimilar passages from quite different novels. The use of one such technique can be seen in the above passage.

Do you remember how in *Hard Times* Dickens draws attention to the gulf between the world of love and the world of money by having his characters speak very differently? In that novel, the inhabitants of the world of love (represented by Sleary's circus) speak a language which deviates from normal expression. What we can notice in the above passage is that Joe, like Sleary, uses language in a way which is again deviant. This should awaken us to the fact that Joe is in some way outside ordered and conventional society. His view of the world, as the above passage demonstrates, is one based upon a simple love for his fellow men, and this is brought out in the way he speaks a language other than that used by the inhabitants of the world of money. Using this as a springboard into analysis of this passage, we can immediately see that there is a tension between the world of love (represented by Joe), and the world of money (represented by Miss Havisham and Estella). Between these two we find Pip, who is in some way related to both. And this directs our attention to a more specific tension: Pip's relation to Joe, on the one hand, and his relation to Miss Havisham and Estella, on the other.

To pull these ideas together, then, we can say that the tension in this passage is in the relationship between the various characters and Pip, the subject of the transaction. That it is a transaction is well worth keeping in mind, for it is this which provides the focus of the tensions within the passage. These tensions all bear down upon Pip, whom each character regards differently: to Joe, the relationship is simple – he loves Pip dearly; to Miss Havisham, Pip is a utility who has 'earned a premium', and now she has finished with him she is selling him off to another master – 'Give it to your master, Pip', she says, meaning Joe; and to Estella, Pip, whom she now regards from behind Miss Havisham's chair, is an object of disdain, the 'common labouring boy' (p. 89) she treated 'as insolently as if he were a dog in disgrace' (p. 92). Having identified this general tension between the characters in the passage as a whole, the thing to do now is to look at the details of the passage and to consider how these reinforce this tension.

To take Joe's relationship with Pip first. The most striking thing about Joe's response to the situation is that he replies not to Miss Havisham, but to Pip. This in itself is immediately amusing, and there are all sorts of ways in which we can account for it naturalistically. There is every reason to assume that this simple village blacksmith is understandably in awe of this strange woman in her strange house. But, as always, and although we can account for the situation naturalistically, Joe's response also fits in with the thematic tensions of the passage and of the novel as a whole. When Miss Havisham tries to confirm with Joe that he expected 'no premium for the boy', Joe fails to answer. The reason for this is plain: he doesn't answer because he has no answer. As he tells Pip, it 'were not a question requiring an answer betwixt yourself and me'. Joe is unnerved and affronted not only by Miss Havisham's strange appearance, but also by what he sees as her strange desire to turn his relationship with Pip into a commercial one. In refusing to talk directly to Miss Havisham, he is refusing to share in her view of the world, refusing to turn his love for Pip into a commercial transaction.

Miss Havisham and Estella, on the other hand, share in their view of Pip only as an object – a point reinforced by the fact that they both see him, quite literally, from the same position: 'Estella stood at the back of Miss Havisham's chair'. Their relationship to Pip and Joe, signalled by the physical distance between them, is the relationship of master to servant; Miss Havisham, for example, is insistent that – as she says a little later – 'Gargery is your [Pip's] new master now' (p. 130), implying, therefore, that she was his master previously. Just as Joe cannot conceive of a relationship based upon economic principles, so Miss Havisham and Estella are unable to conceive of a relationship based upon love. This conflict has massive implications for Pip's relationship with Joe, and marks a turning-point in his career. This can be seen most obviously in the way Pip describes Joe. Previously, he has told us that his love for Joe was a simple matter of equality: 'I had always treated Joe as a larger species of child, and as no more than my equal' (p. 40). Now, however, that he is the subject of a commercial transaction, and confronted by the world of money represented by Miss Havisham, Pip's simple love for Joe is replaced by shame: 'I am afraid to say I was ashamed of the dear good fellow – I *know* I was ashamed of him.' But not only is Pip ashamed of Joe; he suddenly enters into a new relationship with him, the relationship of master and servant. On the one hand, Joe, as Miss Havisham insists, is Pip's new 'master'; but, on the other, and as Pip now sees Joe, he is a socially inept fool, and somebody to be ashamed of in front of Miss Havisham and Estella. This tension, then, between Pip and Joe, on the one hand, and Pip, Estella and Miss Havisham, on the other, underpins the more general tension in the novel as a whole between the world of love and the world of money, for it is the pernicious effect of money upon people and relationships which destroys the simple love Pip had previously held for Joe.

4   *Select a third passage for discussion*

When Miss Havisham makes Pip Joe's apprentice, she is effectively paying him off for his services to her. But Pip, because of a series of coincidences regarding Jaggers, has a secret belief that she will one day make it possible for him to become a gentleman and marry Estella. That she has no such intention only serves to reinforce the revenge that she is exacting upon Pip through Estella. But the effect of Estella upon Pip, and the effect of his delusions about Miss Havisham's intentions, make him increasingly dissatisfied with his life at the forge, and with his lowly station as a blacksmith's apprentice. In the fourth year of this apprenticeship, Mr Jaggers arrives from London, bringing news of Pip's great expectations:

'My name,' he said, 'is Jaggers, and I am a lawyer in London. I am pretty well known. I have unusual business to transact with you, and I commence by explaining that it is not of my originating. If my advice had been asked, I should not have been here. It was not asked, and you see me here. What I have to do as the confidential agent of another, I do. No less, no more.'

Finding that he could not see us very well from where he sat, he got up, and threw one leg over the back of a chair and leaned upon it; thus having one foot on the seat of the chair, and one foot on the ground.

'Now, Joseph Gargery, I am the bearer of an offer to relieve you of this young fellow your apprentice. You would not object to cancel his indentures, at his request and for his good? You would want nothing for so doing?'

'Lord forbid that I should want anything for not standing in Pip's way,' said Joe, staring.

'Lord forbidding is pious, but not to the purpose,' returned Mr Jaggers. 'The question is, Would you want anything? Do you want anything?'

'The answer is,' returned Joe sternly, 'No.'

I thought Mr Jaggers glanced at Joe, as if he considered him a fool for his disinterestedness. But I was too much bewildered between breathless curiosity and surprise, to be sure of it.

'Very well,' said Mr Jaggers. 'Recollect the admission you have made, and don't try to go from it presently.'

'Who's a-going to try?' retorted Joe.   (p. 164)

The basic tension we can see in this passage is a simple one: love on the one side, money on the other. Certainly it is easy to detect in Joe's manner his adherence to his feelings for Pip, and in Jaggers's manner his adherence to the facts of the case; Joe is adamant that he will not stand in Pip's way, and refuses to accept any money for releasing him from his apprenticeship (' "The answer is," returned Joe sternly, "No" '); Jaggers is equally adamant that he is merely carrying out the actions of another ('What I have to do as the confidential agent of another, I do. No less, no more'). What is interesting is not so much the simple honesty with which Joe responds to the suggestion that Pip be made the subject of a commercial transaction, but rather the simple honesty with which Jaggers carries out his business. Between the two it is possible to notice a subtle piece of information being conveyed by the text about Pip himself.

But to take Joe first. The situation in which Joe finds himself would seem to be identical to that in which he found himself with Miss Havisham in the previous passage: he is being made a financial offer regarding Pip. But Joe is altogether more confident in this passage. He answers Jaggers directly, 'sternly', and not *through* Pip, as he did when questioned by Miss Havisham. Jaggers, on the other side, is equally straightforward: 'I have unusual business to transact with you, and I commence by explaining that it is not of my originating. If my advice had been asked, I should not have been here.' Clearly, Jaggers is merely carrying out the orders of another and nothing more.

Now, what we have here is an interesting situation involving two apparently diametrically opposed characters, one devoted to the world of feelings and love, the other devoted to the world of facts and evidence. What the passage does, however, is illustrate that these two characters are in a way very similar. They are clearly devoted to two opposed systems, but they serve those systems honestly. Of course, Jaggers has always received something of a bad press from critics, but the evidence of the text demonstrates that he is a wholly trustworthy person, reliable and efficient, and devoted to carrying out his clients' instructions. He may not like the system in which he works – a point reinforced by the way in which he is constantly washing his hands with strong-smelling soap, as if to wash himself clean of the corrupt world with which he deals – but his work in it is carried out with scrupulous attention and devoted honesty.

What this seems to suggest is that Joe and Jaggers para-doxically share in a fundamental honesty. The systems in which they work are different, but there is a natural sympathy between them – a point emphasised by Jaggers' standing with one foot on the floor and one foot on the chair, as if to suggest this link between the two characters; Jaggers does not view Joe from the safety of his chair (as Miss Havisham and Estella did in the previous passage), but recognises his proximity to him. And, indeed, if we think about the two characters as two sides of the same coin, we can begin to see some interesting parallels between them. Before the novel opens, both men have come across a woman with a child, and both respond according to their view of the world: Joe married Mrs Joe to provide love for her and the child, Pip; Jaggers had the child Estella adopted, to save her mother from the gallows. Although they respond differently, they both respond in the best way that their view of the world allows. Similarly, when Pip goes to London, Jaggers replaces Joe as the epitome of the type of society represented by money and facts, just as Joe had previously been the epitome of the world represented by simple love. In a sense, Joe and Jaggers function as unchanging symbols of the two worlds of love and money, and this explains why it is that they seem never to age, while Pip most clearly does. In London, this conflict between love and money is brought together in the character of Wemmick, who, strangely balanced between Little Britain and Newgate, leads two quite separate lives. But this is something that Pip never achieves, simply because he does not understand the integrity of both Joe and Jaggers to the systems they represent.

This idea – that Pip fails to understand the integrity of each character – is given to us in a subtle form in the above passage. Watching the exchange between Joe and Jaggers, Pip is unsure how to interpret what he sees: 'I thought Mr Jaggers glanced at Joe, as if he considered him a fool for his disinterestedness. But I was too much bewildered between breathless curiosity and surprise, to be sure of it.' What you should notice here is the use of phrases which indicate how uncertain Pip is of what passes between the two men: 'I thought ... as if ... But I was too much bewildered ... to be sure of it.' The reason why he is uncertain is that he does not understand the nature of these two men; he fails to understand the simple love of which Joe is the epitome, and he fails to understand Jaggers's integrity to the world of facts and money. Consequently, when he does go to London, he falls between the two worlds of Joe on the one hand and Jaggers on the other and becomes a worthless snob. He cuts himself off from Joe and the love he can offer, but, unlike Jaggers, he fails to understand the consequences of being a part of the world of money: isolation from others, loneliness and lovelessness.

What I am hoping at this point is that you will wildly disagree with my reading of Jaggers, and be able to think of plenty of passages to analyse which will contradict everything I have said. It doesn't matter whether you agree with me: it is more important that you try out some analyses for yourself and build your own reading of the novel. But whatever you prove or disprove, make sure that you do it by analysing passages and by demonstrating how they enable you to draw certain conclusions. The central thing to remember is that the basic conflict in a Dickens novel is going to be between love on the one hand and money on the other, as in the next passage, which is a stormy interview between Estella and Miss Havisham.

5   Select a fourth passage for discussion

In comparison to the sort of honesty and integrity that I see in Jaggers, Miss Havisham's manipulation of Estella's character is clearly destructive. The following scene occurs at Satis House, where Pip has been asked to accompany Estella.

We were seated by the fire, as just now described, and Miss Havisham still had Estella's arm drawn through her own, and still clutched Estella's hand in hers, when Estella gradually began to detach herself. She had shown a proud impatience more than once before, and had rather endured that fierce affection than accepted or returned it.

'What!' said Miss Havisham, flashing her eyes upon her, 'are you tired of me?'

'Only a little tired of myself,' replied Estella, disengaging her arm, and moving to the great chimney-piece, where she stood looking down at the fire.

'Speak the truth, you ingrate!' cried Miss Havisham, passionately striking her stick upon the floor; 'you are tired of me.'

Estella looked at her with perfect composure, and again looked down at the fire. Her graceful figure and her beautiful face expressed a self-possessed indifference to the wild heat of the other, that was almost cruel.

'You stock and stone!' exclaimed Miss Havisham. 'You cold, cold heart!'

'What?' said Estella, preserving her attitude of indifference as she leaned against the great chimney-piece and only moving her eyes; 'do you reproach me for being cold? You?'

'Are you not?' was the fierce retort.

'You should know,' said Estella. 'I am what you have made me. Take all the praise, take all the blame; take all the success, take all the failure; in short, take me.' (pp. 321–2)

The tension in this passage has to do with the conflict between the burning passion of Miss Havisham and the cold indifference of Estella. This is presented in such a way as to reverse the natural order of things: Estella, young, beautiful and attractive – attributes which we normally associate with the passion of youth – is standing near the fire, and yet presents nothing but a cold, uncaring and unloving character; Miss Havisham, old and wizened like a witch, is paradoxically burning with passion. We can identify this conflict in the language used to describe the two women. Estella is 'proud', she 'endures' Miss Havisham's affection, she possesses 'perfect composure', but also a 'self-possessed indifference' which is 'almost cruel', she leans impassive against the chimney-piece 'only moving her eyes'. Miss Havisham, on the other hand, craves Estella's contact with a 'fierce affection', her eyes 'flash', she 'passionately' strikes her stick upon the floor. The contradiction is that Estella cannot feel the passion which is destroying Miss Havisham, because Miss Havisham has destroyed it in her. What we therefore see is a reversal of the natural order which draws attention to the destructive way in which Miss Havisham has manipulated Estella's character.

The whole point of the passage is to reveal to the reader the extent of the destruction of any normal capacity for love in Estella by Miss Havisham; but the irony of the passage is that Miss Havisham needs the very love she has destroyed. It is Miss Havisham who 'clutched Estella's hand in hers', a hopelessly passionate grasp from which Estella 'gradually began to detach herself'. All Estella can do is what her name suggests – reflect, like the cold star from which her name is derived, a beauty devoid of any natural warmth of its own.

What happens here to Miss Havisham is what happens to Pip in the novel as a whole: Miss Havisham, like Pip, confuses wealth and love. She has given Estella everything that money can give: clothes, jewels, the ability to break men's hearts – but she has given her all this within the cold, isolated and distorting world of Satis House, cut off from the light of day and from the warmth and love that should characterise humanity. In creating Estella, Miss Havisham has created a cold automaton, incapable either of receiving or of giving love. The irony is that she has destroyed the very love she most craves. This is the point which is made in Estella's final speech: 'Take all the praise, take all the blame; take all the success, take all the failure; in short, take me.' But the full implication of this speech does not come out easily. It will be worthwhile to consider this speech very carefully and to analyse precisely how it achieves its effect, because it makes use of several devices characteristic of Dickens's style and will help in your analysis of other Dickens novels.

First, it is important to notice the use of punctuation, and how this speech achieves its effect almost poetically. The device of repeating phrases, as this speech does, is known technically as anaphoric repetition, and its effect is to foreground or draw attention to a specific point. It works by deleting part of the grammatical order of the sentence, in this case the subject 'you'. If we insert this deleted 'you', then the meaning of the speech begins to come clear: '[You] take all the praise, [you] take all the blame; [you] take all the success, [you] take all the failure; in short, [you] take me.' What this implies is a logical pattern of argument, indicated by the repetition of phrases and the caesural effect of the semi-colon separating the phrases. To make real sense of the speech, therefore, we need to insert the markers of logical argument: '[If you] take all the praise, [then you must also] take all the blame; [if you] take all the success, [then you must also] take all the failure; in short, [you must] take me [as you have made me].' This, then, is the full meaning of the speech. Miss Havisham has made Estella by destroying the child's capacity to love, and it is therefore unreasonable for Miss Havisham to complain if Estella cannot love her. And yet it is this very desire for love which Miss Havisham most craves, having been unable to destroy it in herself. Much later in the novel, Miss Havisham will spontaneously combust; the 'wild heat' of her own passion will ultimately destroy her, because she has turned her own capacity to love into mere passion, and, more specifically, into hate. What Dickens seems to be suggesting is that, while the capacity to love is a redeeming characteristic of humanity, that same passion, when used as a threat or bargaining-tool to manipulate another person, is ultimately destructive both of the person who is manipulated, and of the person who does the manipulating. Miss Havisham's spite turns love into hatred, and the natural order is destroyed.

6   *Have I achieved a sufficiently complex sense of the novel?*

One of the things that we can see already is that the novel explores the many facets of the relationships that exist between people. It does this by setting love in conflict with money, and demonstrates the pernicious effect of money upon people and upon their ability to care for another person. What makes the novel particularly interesting, however, is that in exploring the nature of love between people it is able to explore some of the darker areas of the human mind, because love itself operates irrationally. For example, there is a great deal in Miss Havisham with which we can sympathise, because we know the sadness of her past. But it is in her response to the past that we lose sympathy with her. In a sense, she attempts to rationalise a situation which is really beyond rationalisation. Consequently, she chooses to use love – in her case thwarted love – as a lever upon other people, and to use love in this way is ultimately destructive.

   What is worth remembering is that much the same is going to be true even of minor characters in the novel, such as Orlick and Mrs Joe. Mrs Joe is forever reminding Pip how fortunate he is to have been brought up 'by hand', and how many sacrifices she has made on his behalf, reinforcing these sacrifices with the necessary application of 'Tickler', a wax-ended piece of cane. The following confrontation between Mrs Joe, Tickler and Pip demonstrates the point:

> 'Where have you been, you young monkey?' said Mrs Joe, stamping her foot. 'Tell me directly what you've been doing to wear me away with fret and fright and worrit, or I'd have you out of that corner if you was fifty Pips, and he was five hundred Gargerys.'
>
> 'I have only been to the churchyard,' said I, from my stool, crying and rubbing myself.
>
> 'Churchyard!' repeated my sister. 'If it warn't for me you'd have been to the churchyard long ago, and stayed there. Who brought you up by hand?'
>
> 'You did,' said I.
>
> 'And why did I do it, I should like to know?' exclaimed my sister. I whimpered, 'I don't know.'
>
> 'I don't!' said my sister. 'I'd never do it again! I know that. I may truly say I've never had this apron of mine off, since born you were. It's bad enough to be a blacksmith's wife (and him a Gargery) without being your mother.'
>
> My thoughts strayed from that question as I looked disconsolately at the fire. For, the fugitive out on the marshes with the ironed leg, the mysterious young man, the file, the food, and the dreadful pledge I was under to commit a larceny on those sheltering premises, rose before me in the avenging coals.
>
> (p. 41)

This scene occurs directly after Pip's meeting with Magwitch in the churchyard, a scene which demonstrates Pip's isolation in the world, and his desire for parental love. The contrast between Pip's need for parental love and a home, and this confrontation with Mrs Joe, his adoptive mother in her home, sums up much of what the novel is about: characters are alone in the world and need the love and affection of others, but this must be freely given, not bought by money or forced out by threats.

We can see here, however, that Mrs Joe expects Pip's gratitude and love, without expending any herself – just as Miss Havisham expects Estella's love, even after having killed Estella's capacity for love. What all this is based upon is love by reward, love with a price-tag on it. It works through the operation of guilt, and Pip senses this guilt keenly: 'the pledge I was under to commit a larceny on those sheltering premises, rose before me in the avenging coals'. Mrs Joe's method is emotional blackmail plain and simple, and, just as distorted passion eventually destroys Miss Havisham, so Mrs Joe is eventually killed by the same distorted passion. It is this which, much later, Orlick, 'shaking his head and hugging himself' (p. 435), tells us drove him to attempt to kill both

Mrs Joe and Pip: 'You [Pip] was favoured, and he [Orlick] was bullied and beat' (p. 437). Even the lowly Orlick craves love, and, in being deprived of it, his craving turns into violence and hatred. Or, at least, that is the conclusion I draw. Your examination of the evidence might lead you to see things differently. What I do hope is plain by this stage, however, is that the analytic method illustrated here is very simple and straightforward, concentrating attention on specific passages of the text. It is only when you concentrate on passages from the novel in this way that you begin to see both the complexity of the novel as a whole, and the way in which characters and situations interconnect thematically. The controlling principle all the time is to keep to a few ideas, then interpret the details in the light of those ideas, and steadily you should find yourself constructing your own coherent view of the novel.

II Aspects of the novel

What I have tried to do so far is to illustrate a method by which you can begin to sort out the details of what is a fairly complicated novel. This has meant looking at particular extracts which tell us something about certain characters and themes in *Great Expectations*. But what I want to look at now is how the novel presents its story.

For example, if you think about the type of story Pip seems to be telling, it would seem to be a classic Victorian love story: poor boy meets and falls in love with a rich girl, and, after various trials and tribulations, a will is discovered (in *Great Expectations* the secret benefaction) which enables the poor boy to marry the rich girl. That this is the type of story Pip wants to tell underlines the extent of his own delusions about himself, Miss Havisham and Estella: if Miss Havisham had intended Pip to marry Estella she would hardly have apprenticed him as a blacksmith in the first place; Estella is unable to love him or anybody; and it is only *after* the loss of his expectations that he and Estella are united. Finally, the idea of a love story which brings into harmony two characters who are otherwise separated by money, class and background is indicative of Pip's desire to find some kind of order in the confusion of life. In his desire to find such order Pip readily acquiesces to the manipulation of his own life by Miss Havisham, whom he believes is his secret benefactress.

As we have seen, this manipulation of character is a central theme in *Great Expectations*, springing from the desire to love in a world in which love is constantly frustrated by the power of money. Pip, for example, never intimates that he wants to be morally or spiritually any better than he already is. All he needs – or so he believes – is for Miss Havisham to make him wealthy and therefore a gentleman. That done, he will be a fit object for Estella's love.

But a moral and spiritual change does occur in Pip. What is ironic is that this change occurs not because of his love for Estella, but because of his developing love for Magwitch. Furthermore, Pip's life is manipulated by two people who are curiously related to each other: Miss Havisham and Magwitch.

Miss Havisham and Magwitch never meet, and there is no suggestion that either even knows of the other's existence, but they both manipulate Pip's life in some way. That there is this relationship between them is made plain in the structure of the novel as a whole: they share the same enemy, Compeyson, who betrays them both for money; and Miss Havisham is the adoptive mother of Magwitch's daughter, Estella, which provides a further link between the two characters. Given these structural parallels, it is important to examine how the novel presents their shared relationship with Pip.

In both cases, the manipulation of Pip's life is effected through money. Magwitch wants to make, by virtue of the money he has amassed in Australia, a 'brought-up London gentleman' (p. 339); Miss Havisham wants to make, by virtue of her money and the jewels she hangs on Estella, a lady to break the hearts of men. That is, money creates a system in which people will buy their possession of another person's life, in recompense for the love they cannot have, because the result of not having love is isolation. Miss Havisham, jilted on her wedding-day for money, has lived cut off from the light of day ever since; Magwitch, deserted and branded by society as 'a terrible hardened one' (p. 361), betrayed by Compeyson for money, has likewise lived cut off from society in prisons and finally Australia. But Magwitch cannot resist the temptation to return to England, even at the risk of his own life, to gloat over the gentleman he has 'made', just as Miss Havisham cannot resist the temptation to gloat over Estella's effect on Pip. Both characters have been denied love, and both attempt to exact revenge because of it. Their attempt to experience vicariously through Estella and Pip the lives they should have had is initially just an act of revenge. They can now do, through the characters whose lives they manipulate, what society has done to them. What Dickens seems to be suggesting is that this desire for revenge is not only destructive of the internal, spiritual nature of the individual, but actually generated by society itself.

It is important to remember that this desire for revenge is generated by society, the world of money, because in the case of both Miss Havisham and Magwitch, love overcomes it. Miss Havisham's last words to Pip are indicative of her recognition of what she has done to him to satisfy her desire for revenge, but also of his compassion for her: 'Take the pencil and write under my name, "I forgive her"' (p. 415). Magwitch dies similarly contrite, his revenge swallowed up by Pip's developing love for him. In a sense, both characters have to die to achieve forgiveness for what they have done not to society as a whole, but to the emotions of other individuals.

It is important to recognise, however, that the manipulation of Pip's life by Magwitch and Miss Havisham is thematically and structurally at one with the novel as a whole; love, as it is seen through the characters of Magwitch and Miss Havisham and their relationships with Pip, is ultimately destructive, although both characters do experience a death-bed conversion. Set against this, we find the love story of Pip and Estella, which should demonstrate the positive side of love, acting as a touchstone against which the thwarted passion of Miss Havisham and Magwitch can be tested. This is how Pip describes his love for Estella:

The unqualified truth is, that when I loved Estella with the love of a man, I loved her simply because I found her irresistible. Once for all; I knew to my sorrow, often and often, if not always, that I loved her against reason, against promise, against peace, against hope, against happines, against all discouragement that could be. (pp. 253–4)

Truly it was impossible to dissociate her presence from all those wretched hankerings after money and gentility that had disturbed my boyhood – from all those ill-regulated aspirations that had first made me ashamed of home and Joe – from all those visions that had raised her face in the glowing fire, struck it out of the iron on the anvil, extracted it from the darkness of night to look in at the wooden window of the forge and flit away. In a word, it was impossible for me to separate her, in the past or in the present, from the innermost life of my life. (p. 257)

It is the complete and utter abandonment of Pip to Estella which makes such an effect in these passages. Estella has become a part of Pip's very soul, a part of his 'innermost life', from which he can never escape. Pip can find no rational side to his love for her; he loves her simply because she is 'irresistible' to him; he loves her 'against reason, against promise, against peace, against hope, against happiness, against all discouragement that could be.' This is a deep spiritual confusion and abandonment, in which Pip gives himself over to uncontrollable passion. As if to stress the extent to which Pip is subject to Estella's phantom-like nature, she is described in terms of a 'vision', which materialises in the 'glowing fire', lurks in 'the darkness of the night', and 'flits away' from the forge window. This is love of a type which is wholly destructive. It is love of a type that should be feared, born, as Pip says, out of his 'wretched hankerings after money and gentility', and this is indicative of the conflict between the individual and society at large. The personal turmoil Pip finds in his love for Estella, motivated by his desire for 'money and gentility', serves to mirror the conflicts in the individual's relationship to the outside world. So even in the love story of Pip and Estella, which reads on the surface much like any other Victorian love story, we find deep spiritual and emotional turmoil, which reflects the untidiness and turmoil of society at large.

This turmoil in Pip's character and in his relationship to the outside world is given focus toward the end of the novel when, having recovered from a long illness, through which he was nursed by the loving Joe, Pip determines to put his life in order by returning to the forge and asking Biddy to marry him. There is clearly a high degree of snobbery in Pip, even at this late stage of the novel, in his willingness to give himself up to Biddy, who is so far beneath him socially. But the irony is that Pip arrives at the forge only to discover that Biddy has married Joe. This marriage between Biddy and Joe is the final nail in the coffin of Pip's expectations: he is denied the cosy domesticity of love represented by Biddy, and he is denied the wildly passionate love which he craves with Estella. So Pip's confusion is finally increased by his snobbish decision to give himself to Biddy, since events again conspire against him. This reinforces the idea that the emotions are not a tidy collection of events arranged to make sense, but are instead random, complicated and unfathomable; and the same seems true of the world at large.

This sense of instability is reinforced by Dickens's choice of a first-person narrator. First-person narrators are notoriously unstable narrators, simply because the reader is never quite sure of the truthfulness of their report. Many first-person narrators, for example, tell lies about themselves and the situations they report, in order to disturb the reader's cosy relationship with the story. But Dickens chooses not to use his narrator in this way. Instead, he has Pip relate his story in a historic perspective, looking back over the events of his life, quite aware of his own failings at certain points in the story, and willing to point these out to the reader. It is quite true that Pip does deceive himself in the process of coming into his expectations. But it is equally true that he makes no attempt to deceive the reader, and that consequently, looking back over his life, he is aware of his own self-deception: 'All other swindlers upon earth are nothing to the self-swindlers, and with such pretences did I cheat myself' (p. 247).

To use a first-person narrator in this way tells us a great deal both about the novel and about Dickens's motivation in writing the story. First, when Dickens could so easily add to the general confusion of the emotional and physical world he describes, he uses his narrator instead as a touchstone of stability: what Pip has experienced may have confused him emotionally, but he relates that in a meaningful and ordered way. Secondly, this increases our sense that we are being told a story, simply because we know that life generally refuses to arrange itself in the coherent patterns that we find in a novel. And this in turn reinforces our awareness that the emotions and the world at large, when unfiltered by the story teller's art, are random and largely resistant to our comprehension.

Having said that, the ending of the novel itself appears to deny the untidiness of the emotional world which Dickens has previously been describing. The novel ends by uniting Pip and Estella in the ruins of Satis House, with the implicit promise of marriage and happiness in the future. As you may know, Dickens originally planned to have Pip and Estella meet and part, presumably forever, but another nineteenth-century novelist, Bulwer-Lytton, persuaded Dickens to change the ending to the one we now have.

It would be possible to construct some fairly persuasive arguments about which is the more satisfying of the two endings. In the original ending, for example, Pip is the confirmed loser, Biddy having married the blacksmith he would have been; in the second ending, an ideal order is created, and Pip is given another chance for happiness. I don't intend to become involved in the argument about which is the better ending of the two, but we can see how the whole question of how to end such a novel as *Great Expectations* can arise in the first place, and this can tell us a great deal about the nature of the novel and novel-writing. In a sense, the story has to be resolved at the end of the novel because, although part of the novelist's job is to make us aware of the disorder and muddle of life, another aspect of the novelist's job is to create order, to arrange life into a coherent and meaningful story. Indeed, the idea that a novel tells a story in the first place suggests that it is possible to arrange the complexities, the randomness and the muddle of life into coherence. But, when Dickens came to the end of *Great Expectations* and had to decide what was going to happen to Pip and Estella, he was faced with trying to reconcile not just the ambiguities and complexities of Pip's story, but also the ambiguities and complexities of society at large, of which Pip's story is a reflection.

Wherever we look in the novel, we can find this same pattern in which the personal conflicts in the individual's life are a reflection of the conflicts to be found in society at large. After Magwitch has been betrayed by Compeyson and recaptured, he is brought before the judge to be sentenced along with thirty-one other prisoners:

The sun was striking in at the great windows of the court, through the glittering drops of rain upon the glass, and it made a broad shaft of light between the two and thirty and the Judge, linking both together, and perhaps reminding some among the audience, how both were passing on, with absolute equality, to the greater Judgement that knoweth all things and cannot err. Rising for a moment, a distinct speck of face in this way of light, the prisoner said, 'My Lord, I have received my sentence of Death from the Almighty, but I bow to yours,' and sat down again. There was some hushing, and the Judge went on with what he had to say to the rest. Then, they were all formally doomed, and some of them were supported out, and some of them sauntered out with a haggard look of bravery, and a few nodded to the gallery, and two or three shook hands, and others went out chewing the fragments of herb they had taken from the sweet herbs lying about. He went last of all, because of having to be helped from his chair and to go very slowly; and he held my hand while all the others were removed, and while the audience got up (putting their dresses right, as they might at church or elsewhere) and pointed down at this criminal or that, and most of all at him and me.

(pp. 467–8)

The first thing we notice about this passage is what a marvellous piece of writing it is, and how it is really quite unnerving, verging, as it does, almost on the comic. And yet, tied in with this unnerving, almost comic aspect of the writing, the passage also further develops the novel's broader thematic concerns. We notice, for example, the high degree of sympathy between Pip and Magwitch. When Magwitch had first arrived at Pip's lodgings, Pip told us that 'the repugnance with which I shrank from him, could not have been exceeded if he had been some terrible beast' (p. 337), but here Pip holds Magwitch's hand and helps him from his chair. We know what has happened to Pip by this point in the story: 'my repugnance to him had all melted away ... I only saw a man who had meant to be my benefactor ... I only saw in him a much better man than I had been to Joe' (pp. 456–7). Pip has realised, through his developing love for Magwitch, that his pretensions to social rank, made on the basis of Magwitch's money, served only to isolate him even further by making him unable to love. Now that his repugnance for Magwitch has 'melted away' he can see the superficiality of the social world, and yet its dreadful power to control lives.

This is the conflict at the centre of the above passage. On the one hand, society is a mere façade; on the other, it has the power to control lives utterly, even to end them. The whole proceedings are imbued with a sense of theatricality, of spectacle and social ritual; the criminals stand before the spectators in the 'gallery', playing out their pathetic roles to the end: 'they were all formally doomed, and some of them were supported out, and some of them sauntered out with a haggard look of bravery, and a few nodded to the gallery, and two or three shook hands ...' Meanwhile, the 'audience' responds with a show of social ritual, 'putting their dresses right, as they might at church or elsewhere'.

The effect gained by this technique is extremely unnerving, since the whole show is almost funny in the pathetically grand gestures the criminals attempt to present to the world. And yet the scene it describes is one in which more than thirty people are being condemned to death – which is manifestly not funny. The passage achieves this unnerving effect by describing the scene in a way which seems wholly inappropriate to what is actually happening. The criminals are all 'formally doomed' by the Judge; some of the criminals 'sauntered out', while others 'nodded to the gallery'. By describing the scene in the way he does, Dickens is able to take a sideways look at it, to see it for what it is. And it is this which gives us the sense of the ridiculous nature of such proceedings. Dickens refuses to accept the validity of conventions which most of us usually accept without question, and he does this by describing the situation in a quite literal way. It is ridiculous that these thirty people can be sentenced to death by some old judge sniffing at a nosegay. But that is exactly what happens. By describing the scene in the irreverently literal way that he does, Dickens is able to draw attention to the façade that society utilises to construct its rules and account for its behaviour. But by keeping his distance from it, and by describing it in the way he does, Dickens is refusing to co-operate in the idea that the law court is anything other than an elaborate and nonsensical charade.

This is reinforced by the way in which the criminals are described in the most anonymous terms: even Magwitch, who we have by now come to know very well, is described merely as 'a distinct speck of face in this way of light'. This sense of anonymity not only of Magwitch but also of the thirty or so other prisoners reinforces the idea that these characters are merely acting out roles in an uncaring society, and this increases our strong sense of indignation at the treatment of these 'formally doomed' and helpless characters. What increases the effect of the passage still further, however, is that it unnerves us by showing just what a charade the whole show really is. And this is really very similar to what we are made to feel about Pip's abandonment to his love for Estella. This charade of justice is a system out of control, a system over which the individual has no control whatsoever, just as Pip has no control over his deep need to love Estella 'once for all'. Both Pip's abandonment in his love for Estella, and the disruptive, unnerving way in which Dickens reports the court scene, are indicative of the confusions, ambiguities and contradictions in society itself.

What I want finally to consider is how Dickens puts together this deep sense of uncontrolled confusion in the individual and society. The first thing to remember is that *Great Expectations* is an enormously humorous novel. Pip, in the process of stealing food for Magwitch, slips a piece of bread and butter into his trousers. The adult Pip recalls: 'Conscience is a dreadful thing when it accuses man or boy; but when, in the case of a boy, that secret burden co-operates with another secret burden down the leg of his trousers, it is (as I can testify) a great punishment' (p. 44).

The detached way in which this is reported by the adult Pip allows the reader to savour the gradual unrolling of the description, the drawing-together of the psychological burden of conscience with the very real burden of a piece of bread and butter down the trouser-leg. In a similar way, Pip recalls the medicinal application of Tar-water which his sister forced him to take: 'At the best of times, so much of this elixir was administered to me as a choice restorative, that I was conscious of going about, smelling like a new fence' (p. 44). Again, the detached, reporting tone of the piece creates much of the humour, and this is added to by the drawing-together of two otherwise unconnected ideas. The Tar-water is described ironically as an 'elixir' and a 'choice restorative', and this pulls together the boy, Pip, on the one hand, and the idea of a newly creosoted fence on the other. Later, Joe is described as looking 'like a scarecrow in good circumstances' (p. 54); for his Christmas lunch, Pip is regaled with 'those obscure corners of pork of which the pig, when living, had had the least reason to be vain' (p. 56); the sergeant searching for Magwitch, having partaken of the rum offered by Pumblechook, parts from him as from a comrade, although Pip doubts 'if he were quite as fully sensible of that gentleman's merits under arid conditions, as when something moist was going' (p. 64); Joe, recalling the death of his parents, rubs 'first one of his eyes, and then the other, in a most uncongenial and uncomfortable manner, with the round knob on the top of the poker' (p. 77).

This ability to surprise the reader by drawing together two things in an unexpected way underpins Dickens's ability to see the funny side of things not usually regarded as funny. Pip speaks, for example, of Mr Wopsle's great-aunt as having 'conquered a confirmed habit of living into which she had fallen' (p. 150), meaning, of course, that she had died – which is not particularly humorous in itself.

Much of Dickens's technique, then, centres on this ability to see things from a shifted perspective, but a perspective which we can immediately recognise as being true, or with which we can immediately sympathise. When Pip steals out of his home to take food to Magwitch he tells us, 'The mist was heavier yet when I got out on the marshes, so that instead of my running at everything, everything seemed to run at me' (p. 48). The truth of that observation is immediately obvious to anyone who has run through mist, but it is Dickens who points it out to us, allowing us, as it were, to rediscover what we may already know, to see things anew. The lens through which Dickens filters this renewed perception is a comic one. But the comic, simply because it does force us to see things for what they really are, is not merely humorous. The comic perspective, as Dickens uses it, allows us to see beneath the façade of the social world, forces us to recognise the craziness of society, the irrational impulses which motivate human beings, and consequently presents what is potentially a highly disruptive view of the world.

Think, for example, of Wemmick, who, with his house cut off from the outside world by a moat and drawbridge, his cosy domestic love with Miss Skiffens, his caring love for his aged parent, seems to represent the ultimate in order, in security and in the tidiness of emotions. But Wemmick achieves this only by physically cutting himself off from the rest of humanity. Even within the cosy domesticity of Wemmick's life with Miss Skiffens and the aged P there are shadows lurking, a sense that order and emotional tidiness is achieved at too great a cost. Similarly, in *Great Expectations* as a whole, the individual is confronted by emotions, such as Pip's love for Estella, which he cannot control; or confronted with a system, such as the sham of the court which sentences Magwitch, too massive and irrational to be controlled either.

At the centre of *Great Expectations* is, then, a comic and disruptive view of the world which recognises the proximity of comedy to human tragedy, and recognises, too, the proximity of the emotional life of the individual to the influences of the outside world. By presenting Pip's love for Estella as being ultimately uncontrollable, and by paralleling that with a comic, sideways glance at the systems and structures within which society organises itself, and within which the individual attempts to organise his response to the world, Dickens presents us with a novel which is both comic and highly disruptive. Consequently, *Great Expectations* is able to hint, even within the comedy, at the darker, and largely irrational impulses that motivate human beings.

4

Bleak House

I Constructing an overall analysis

Bleak House is well over 300,000 words long. This doesn't make it the longest novel in English literature by any means, but it does make it a difficult novel for many students. The thing to remember, however, is to set about analysing the novel in exactly the same way as described in the previous chapters. In fact, with a novel as long as *Bleak House*, it is even more important to proceed step by step with your analysis. As always, the place to start is with the story.

1 *After reading the novel, think about the story and what kind of pattern you can see in the text*

Bleak House deals with an apparently interminable Chancery suit – 'Jarndyce and Jarndyce' – and with the characters involved in the suit. The major characters are Ada Clare and Richard Carstone, wards of their kind, elderly relative, John Jarndyce. The other major character is Esther Summerson, a young girl whose schooling was paid for by John Jarndyce, and who is now taken into his household as housekeeper and companion to Ada Clare. Richard and Ada fall in love and secretly marry. They marry secretly because Richard has become obsessed with the Jarndyce suit, even to the extent of distrusting his guardian and benefactor, John Jarndyce. Richard's health gradually declines because of his obsession with the suit. When a new will is discovered, and the suit finally settled, it is found that the whole estate has been swallowed up in legal costs. This is the final blow to Richard's failing health, and he dies.

Running parallel to this story is the narration of Esther Summerson, told in the first person, in retrospect, after a lapse of seven or eight years. This is the story of Lady Dedlock, who is Esther's mother as the result of a youthful relationship with a Captain Hawdon. Hawdon is supposed to have perished at sea, but is actually working as a scrivener. When Lady Dedlock sees his handwriting on a legal document, she realises he is still alive and is thrown into some confusion, a confusion noted by her husband's solicitor, Tulkinghorn. Hawdon dies shortly afterwards, and Lady Dedlock secretly goes to visit his grave. She believes that the secret of her past is safe, but when it is uncovered by a law clerk, Guppy, Lady Dedlock is forced to make herself known to Esther. Later she becomes a murder suspect when Tulkinghorn, who has also divined her secret and intends to tell her husband, is murdered. Learning that her husband has been told her secret by Inspector Bucket, who is investigating Tulkinghorn's murder, Lady Dedlock flies from the house in despair, and is found dead near Hawdon's grave, despite the efforts of Inspector Bucket and Esther to find her. Meanwhile, Esther has accepted a proposal of marriage from Jarndyce, a proposal she has accepted out of her devotion and gratitude to him. But Jarndyce, discovering that she really loves another man, Allan Woodcourt, surrenders her to him in an act of self-sacrifice, thus allowing them to marry.

It is clear from this summary of the plot that Dickens is setting up a fairly straightforward contrast between a corrupt society (represented by the Chancery suit) and simple love and self-sacrifice (represented by John Jarndyce and Esther). Love and self-sacrifice do triumph in the end, but at considerable human cost. Richard, for example, is so obsessed by the Chancery suit that he is eventually killed by it. Similarly, any money that could have come out of the settlement of the case is swallowed up by the legal fees of the case itself, leaving only the lawyers any better off. This promises to be an immensely pessimistic analysis of a corrupt society which quite heedlessly destroys the lives of so many people; yet, as we shall see, the novel manages to tell its story in a lively, even exuberant way.

2   *Analyse the opening paragraph or two of the novel and try to build on the ideas you have established so far*

This is how the novel opens (page references relate to the Penguin edition, 1971):

London. Michaelmas term lately over, and the Lord Chancellor sitting in Lincoln's Inn Hall. Implacable November weather. As much mud in the streets, as if the waters had but newly retired from the face of the earth, and it would not be wonderful to meet a Megalosaurus, forty feet long or so, waddling like an elephantine lizard up Holborn Hill. Smoke lowering down from chimney pots, making a soft black drizzle with flakes of soot in it as big as full-grown snowflakes – gone into mourning, one might imagine, for the death of the sun. Dogs, undistinguishable in mire. Horses scarcely better; splashed to their very blinkers. Foot passengers, jostling one another's umbrellas, in a general infection of ill temper, and losing their foot-hold at street-corners, where tens of thousands of other foot passengers have been slipping and sliding since the day broke (if this day ever broke), adding new deposits to the crust upon crust of mud, sticking at those points tenaciously to the pavement, and accumulating at compound interest.

Fog everywhere. Fog up the river, where it flows among aits and meadows; fog down the river, where it rolls defiled among the tiers of shipping, and the waterside pollutions of a great (and dirty) city. Fog on the Essex marshes, fog on the Kentish heights. Fog creeping into the cabooses of collier-brigs; fog lying out on the yards, and hovering in the rigging of great ships; fog drooping on the gunwhales of barges and small boats. Fog in the eyes and throats of ancient Greenwich pensioners, wheezing by the fireside of their wards; fog in the stem and bowl of the afternoon pipe of the wrathful skipper, down in his close cabin; fog cruelly pinching the toes and fingers of his shivering little 'prentice boy on deck. Chance people on the bridges peeping over the parapets into a nether sky of fog, with fog all round them, as if they were up in a balloon, and hanging in the misty clouds.

Gas looming through the fog in divers places in the streets, much as the sun may, from the spongey fields, be seen to loom by husbandman and ploughboy. Most of the shops lighted two hours before their time – as the gas seems to know, for it has a haggard and unwilling look.

The raw afternoon is rawest, and the dense fog is densest and the muddy streets are muddiest, near that leaden-headed old obstruction, appropriate ornament for the threshold of a leaden-headed old corporation: Temple Bar. And hard by Temple Bar, at the very heart of the fog, sits the Lord High Chancellor in his High Court of Chancery. (p. 49)

This is a highly complex piece of writing which achieves its effects by building up a series of oppositions: the past is opposed to the present; light to dark; the seen to the barely visible; the natural to the defiled. All these oppositions help us to identify the conflict at the centre of the passage: the conflict between the dangerous, threatening and chaotic world represented by the fog and the implicit alternative of a more natural, more humane and ordered world, undefiled by fog and mud.

This conflict is discovered in the details of the passage. The city is hostile and squalid, more the home of a Megalosaurus 'waddling like an elephantine lizard' than a place of human habitation. We find animals in this city, not humans. And the humans we do find seem to be not a natural part of the scene, barely able even to walk through the mud: 'losing their foothold at street-corners ... slipping and sliding'. Further, the fog, which penetrates everything, 'creeping into the cabooses of collier-brigs ... hovering in the rigging of great ships ... in the eyes and throats of ancient Greenwich pensioners ... in the stem and bowl of the afternoon pipe of the wrathful skipper', actually seems to attack human beings physically: 'fog cruelly pinching the toes and fingers of [the] shivering little 'prentice boy on deck'. The effect achieved by this is to suggest how the society in which we are to find the novel's characters is dangerous, destructive and disease-ridden: there is, we are told, 'a general infection of ill-temper'; the skipper, smoking his pipe, is 'wrathful'. This novel is going to be a novel which demonstrates how a corrupt society corrupts, attacks, and eventually destroys its inhabitants.

In such a society, people are pushed into a subsidiary role. We have first of all mud, fog and animals. But no humans. In fact, we seem to be in a world of elemental existence, with humans struggling to survive alongside animals, and even a dinosaur. In these opening paragraphs, we see the primaeval slime out of which the present is created, and in which the novel's characters live their lives. That the novel is returning to the basics of existence is reinforced by the appearance of the four elements: earth, air, fire and water. But each of these is corrupted, serving only to make the details of the world indistinguishable. The air is turned into fog, defiling everything, obscuring everything: 'people on the bridges peeping over the parapets into a nether sky of fog, with fog all around them'. The earth and water are present only as mud, which again serves only to obscure: dogs are 'undistinguishable in mire. Horses, scarcely better; splashed to their very blinkers.' And fire comes 'looming through the fog in divers places', not like the sun which the ploughboy may see 'rising above the fields', but threateningly, wearing 'a haggard and unwilling look'. In the opening paragraphs we are being taken into a world gone wrong, a world in which even the very elements of existence have been corrupted.

The passage continues, as inexorably as the fog itself, seeking out the centre of all this confusion. It finds this centre with the Lord High Chancellor, 'at the very heart of the fog ... in his High Court of Chancery'. The image we have here is suggestive of the spider sitting at the centre of its web, a web in which unsuspecting insects will be caught. The spider will trap them, slowly drain away their life, and eventually devour them. This is precisely how the Court of Chancery works in the novel. The Lord High Chancellor waits like a spider at the centre of a web which connects everything to everything else, and everything and everybody to the Court of Chancery. And this is precisely what we find in the novel as a whole. As we read the novel, we gradually become aware that what at first seemed to be quite unconnected events and characters are in fact uniquely related to other events and characters. Everything turns out to be related to everything else. And everything centres on the Court of Chancery, which waits, trapping characters in its web of tortuous legal procedure. The opening paragraphs of *Bleak House* introduce us to the paralysing, chaotic and destructive inhumanity of Victorian society and its structures, and suggest that people, like insects trapped in the spider's web, will never be able to escape from it.

Any novel with such ideas at its centre promises to be immensely pessimistic. But, as we saw in *Great Expectations,* Dickens's novels are more than just an indictment of society because of his manner of writing and the way in which he tells his stories. Even the opening paragraphs here, whose subject matter is so gloomy, are also extremely entertaining, demonstrating Dickens's sheer enjoyment of language itself. As we progress through the novel, we find many comic characters and situations described with a straightforward exuberance, allowing the reader to savour the ability of language to create a fictional world out of nothing. This is a point to which I can return later, however. For the moment, we leave the primaeval slime of the city behind us, and move into the polite, civilised world of Lady Dedlock.

3 Select a second passage for analysis

My Lady Dedlock has been down at what she calls, in familiar conversation, her 'place' in Lincolnshire. The waters are out in Lincolnshire. An arch of the bridge in the park has been sapped and sopped away. The adjacent low-lying ground, for half a mile in breadth, is a stagnant river, with melancholy trees for islands in it, and a surface punctured all over, all day long, with falling rain. My Lady Dedlock's 'place' has been extremely dreary. The weather, for many a day and night, has been so wet that the trees seem wet through, and the soft loppings and prunings of the woodman's axe can make no crash or crackle as they fall. The deer, looking soaked, leave quagmires, where they pass. The shot of a rifle loses its sharpness in the moist air, and its smoke moves in a tardy little cloud towards the green rise, coppice-topped, that makes a background for the falling rain. The view from my Lady Dedlock's own windows is alternately a lead-coloured view, and a view in Indian ink. The vases on the stone terrace in the foreground catch the rain all day; and the heavy drops fall, drip, drip, drip upon the broad flagged pavement, called, from old time, the Ghost's Walk, all night. On Sundays, the little church in the park is mouldy; the oaken pulpit breaks out into a cold sweat; and there is a general smell and taste as of the ancient Dedlocks in their graves. My Lady Dedlock (who is childless), looking out in the early twilight from her boudoir at a keeper's lodge, and seeing the light of a fire upon the latticed panes, and smoke rising from the chimney, and a child, chased by a woman, running out into the rain to meet the shining figure of a wrapped-up man coming through the gate, has been put quite out of temper. My Lady Dedlock says she has been 'bored to death'.　(p. 56)

Dickens is a master at creating places and landscapes which perfectly mirror the personalities of their inhabitants. We have seen something of this already in the analyses of *Hard Times* and *Great Expectations*, in which the same technique occurs time and again: the descriptions of the Forge and of Satis House in *Great Expectations* serve to tell us a great deal about the warmth of Joe's love and the loneliness and disintegration to be found in Miss Havisham's thwarted passion; Stone Lodge in *Hard Times,* which, 'haunted by the ghost of damp mortar' (p. 59) and its 'deadly statistical clock, which measured every second with a beat like the rap upon a coffin-lid' (p. 132), is a perfect reflection of Gradgrind's dull absorption in facts, just as the 'brazen door-plate, and a brazen door-handle fullstop' (p. 147) outside Bounderby's bank are indicative of the boasting, bullying Bounderby himself. In the above passage, we find this technique being used again, but here to tell us something of the character of Lady Dedlock.

The opposition we perceive in the passage is a subtle one. It centres on the landscape, which is dead and yet a context within which things are happening. This betrays a deep emotional frustration in Lady Dedlock herself, as we shall see. To take the description of the landscape first. We notice, for example, that the natural world seems to be in a state of stagnation: an arch of the bridge has been 'sapped and sopped away'; the river is 'stagnant'; the trees are 'melancholy'; cut trees and branches 'make no crash or crackle as they fall'; the shot of a rifle 'loses its sharpness in the moist air'; the little church in the park is 'mouldy'. Furthermore, the scene is set in Lincolnshire, which is a notoriously flat county, so flat that there seems no sense of distance, with perspective becoming lost in an unending landscape. And yet things are happening in the scene, too. Apart from the rain, part of a bridge has collapsed, a woodman is out lopping trees, deer are wandering in the park, someone is firing a rifle, a keeper returns home to be greeted by his wife and child. The point is that these events are dulled by the atmosphere in which they occur. The picture created by such a scene is one in which things seem to have lost their significance. There seems no meaning to the world, which instead appears purposeless and lost. Things seem only to be waiting for their eventual decay, just as Lady Dedlock seems merely to be waiting to join the family ancestors whose presence we feel seeping out of their tombs: 'there is a general smell and taste as of the ancient Dedlocks in their graves.' Everything seems to have been smoothed out by the rain, so that the flatness of Lincolnshire mirrors the flatness of Lady Dedlock's life. Lady Dedlock's existence (as her name suggests) is as formless, meaningless and paralysed as the world which surrounds her. If in the previous passage we were aware of the chaos of life, in this passage we are made aware of the ordered meaninglessness of life. Just because life at Chesney Wold is steeped in tradition does not automatically confer meaning upon it.

There is, in fact, only one event which catches Lady Dedlock's attention, and it is this which betrays the deep emotional turmoil at the centre of her character: 'looking out in the twilight at a keeper's lodge, and seeing the light of a fire upon the latticed panes, and smoke rising from the chimney, and a child, chased by a woman, running out into the rain to meet the shining figure of a wrapped-up man coming through the gate'. It is this scene which puts her 'quite out of temper', causing her to exclaim that she has been 'bored to death'. Yet it is this scene, too, and her response to it, which tells us most about her. Just preceding this scene we are told that 'My Lady Dedlock ... is childless'. Her response to the homely scene of the keeper's return and of a child running out to greet him consequently raises several questions about her. Is she *bored* by the provincialism of the scene, which is not a part of her fashionable, refined and aloof view of the world? Or is she instead *distressed* by it, because she is forever cut off from sharing in it?

We cannot, of course, answer these questions at this stage of the novel. But in either case the phrase 'bored to death' immediately strikes us as an attempt to put up a façade of some type, a façade which she struggles to maintain to the very end. Similarly, and despite the appearance she attempts to maintain, Lady Dedlock is indissolubly linked in the reader's mind with a child, because, first, the narrator has made a point of telling us that Lady Dedlock is *childless*; and, secondly, it is the appearance of the mother and child which catches her attention and puts her 'quite out of temper'. When Lady Dedlock's child appears, it is Esther Summerson. The façade she has been forced to maintain over so many years, and the attempt she has made to pretend that emotional chaos does not define her ordered existence at Chesney Wold eventually breaks down, and she dies.

4   *Select a third passage for analysis*

> He lived in a pretty house, formerly the Parsonage-house, with a lawn in front, a bright flower-garden at the side, and a well-stocked orchard and kitchen-garden in the rear, enclosed with a venerable wall that had of itself a ripened, ruddy look. But, indeed, everything about the place wore an aspect of maturity and abundance. The old lime-tree walk was like green cloisters, the very shadows of the cherry-trees and apple-trees were heavy with fruit, the gooseberry bushes were so laden that their branches arched and rested on the earth, the strawberries grew in like profusion, and the peaches basked by the hundred on the wall. Tumbled about among the spread nets and the glass frames sparkling and winking in the sun, there were such heaps of drooping pods, and marrows, and cucumbers, that every foot of ground appeared a vegetable treasury, while the smell of sweet herbs and all kinds of wholesome growth (to say nothing of the neighbouring meadows where the hay was carrying) made the whole air a great nosegay. Such stillness and composure reigned within the orderly precincts of the old red wall, that even the feathers hung in garlands to scare the birds hardly stirred; and the wall had such a ripening influence that where, here and there high up, a disused nail and scrap of list still clung to it, it was easy to fancy that they had mellowed with the changing seasons, and that they had rusted and decayed according to the common fate. (p. 301)

It would be difficult to find a passage which contrasts more strongly with Lady Dedlock's view of Lincolnshire than this one, and in it we can find another view of the world, in which life, rather than being formless and without meaning, is instead, purposeful, ordered and fulfilling.

What we notice about the passage is a particular relationship between the past and the present: the present abundance of Boythorn's garden has grown out of a healthy relationship with the past, and this implies a similar relationship to the future also. The past is evident throughout the passage: everything wears 'an aspect of maturity and abundance'; 'stillness and composure reigned within the orderly precincts'; things have 'mellowed with the changing seasons'. What this stresses is an organic growth in nature, and an organic growth which can come only from the past; the present abundance of Boythorn's garden exists only by virtue of the natural pattern of change and decay. It is the garden's relationship with the past which has created its present abundance; and it is the inward strength of this relationship with the past which will guarantee the garden's progression into the future.

This sense of the inward strength and vitality in the garden's present abundance is underpinned by Esther's description, which sets the garden firmly within a religious context. Boythorn's house, for example, had formerly been the 'Parsonage-house'. Even the phrases used to describe the garden are strongly reminiscent of the religious life and of the phraseology of the Bible: the garden is surrounded by 'a venerable wall'; the old lime-tree walk was 'like green cloisters'; the branches 'arched and rested on the earth' forming a natural rainbow, suggestive of the covenant made between God and humanity after the Flood. What all this suggests is that in this garden beauty is to be discovered from within. Just as the 'venerable' monks, walking in silence and seclusion in their monastic 'cloisters' discovered a spiritual beauty within themselves, so Esther discovers an internal beauty in the garden. This is particularly significant when we recall that when Esther sees this garden she is herself recovering from the smallpox, which has left her face terribly scarred. Just as Esther discovers an internal beauty in what she sees in nature, so, by the end of the novel, her own inward beauty appears to make her outwardly beautiful once again, 'prettier than [she] ever [was]' (p. 935).

It is easy to see how the above passage ties in with some of the major thematic concerns of the novel, especially when seen in contrast with the previous passage. What we find in the above passage is the sense of an organic and progressive growth through time to arrive at the present which Esther describes. And here, unlike the passage in which Lady Dedlock figures, where everything is merely waiting for decay and death, we find the natural world in fruition and repose. The trees and fruit are not 'melancholy', as they were in the Dedlock passage, but 'bask' in 'maturity and abundance', confident in 'stillness and composure', 'orderly' and 'mellowed with the changing seasons'. If Lady Dedlock's world is the world of dissolution and ordered chaos in which life is gradually 'sapped and sopped away' to the grave, the world Esther discovers in the garden is one of repose and organic growth into an implied future. The 'common fate' is not, as for those involved with the Court of Chancery and Jarndyce and Jarndyce, a gradual wearing away and eventual death, but is instead a continuing accumulation of strength and vitality into the future. Lady Dedlock and the suitors in Jarndyce and Jarndyce are worn down, their energy slowly sapped away from them until they are dead, and this is the very opposite of the internal beauty and peace that Esther discovers in Boythorn's garden. Esther, like the Esther in the Bible story, is that rare individual: a human being whose character is secure from the rot of wealth, prosperity, and power, secure instead in its natural position within the greater scheme of things.

5   Select a fourth passage for analysis

A general impression of Richard as a weak-willed character is bound to have come across in your initial reading of *Bleak House*. He is unable to stick to any profession and becomes obsessed with the possibility of the fortune that may be waiting for him on the settlement of the Chancery suit. This is the pattern of Richard's life: to await forever some event which will settle things positively for him. The great event for which he waits so long, the settlement of the Chancery suit, at last happens and the whole estate is swallowed up in legal fees. It is only when he is dying that Richard seems to be given that moment of true insight into the nature of things:

> He was lying on a sofa, with his eyes closed, when I went in. There were restoratives on the table; the room was made as airy as possible, and was darkened, and was very orderly and quiet. Allan stood beside him, watching him gravely. His face appeared to me to be quite destitute of colour, and now that I saw him without his seeing me, I fully saw, for the first time, how worn away he was. But he looked handsomer than I had seen him look for many a day.
>
> I sat down by his side in silence. Opening his eyes by and by, he said, in a weak voice, but with his old smile, 'Dame Durden, kiss me, my dear!'
>
> It was a great comfort and surprise to me, to find him in his low state cheerful and looking forward. He was happier, he said, in our intended marriage, than he could find words to tell me. My husband had been a

guardian angel to him and Ada, and he blessed us both, and wished us all the joy that life could yield us. I almost felt as if my own heart would have broken, when I saw him take my husband's hand, and hold it to his breast.

We spoke of the future as much as possible, and he said several times that he must be present at our marriage if he could stand upon his feet. Ada would contrive to take him somehow, he said.   (pp. 924–5)

Certainly, there is a reconciliation in this scene which arises from the contrast between what we know of Richard in the past and how Esther now describes him in the present. Richard had previously suspected John Jarndyce of acting against him in the suit, but here he takes Jarndyce's hand and 'hold[s] it to his breast', acknowledging that he 'had been a guardian angel to him'. The past happy relationship in which they had all shared at Bleak House is also recalled by the way in which Richard addresses Esther: 'Dame Durden, kiss me, my dear!' But beneath all this there is a deep and tragic irony.

Richard's major problem throughout the novel has been to look forward in the belief that some event will signal a change in his life and give it purpose and meaning. Here, the Chancery suit behind him, he begins to build some new event in the future after which everything will be clarified: Esther's marriage. Esther comments, for example, that 'we spoke of the future as much as possible'; 'he was happier, he said, in our intended marriage, than he could find words to tell me'; she is pleased 'to find him cheerful and looking forward'; 'he said several times that he must be present at our marriage'. What we should notice here is how every aspect of Richard's conversation is again 'looking forward' to that illusory future time when all things will be settled, his life set unalterably in order. But this is the same illusory future point to which Richard has been looking throughout the novel, and, despite Esther's assurance that 'the room was orderly and quiet', the reader knows, while Esther appears not to, that Richard's internal life is far from 'orderly and quiet'. He may be fooling Esther, fooling Ada, even fooling himself, but Allan Woodcourt looks on, 'watching him gravely'. Richard will never escape the corrupting influence of the Chancery suit, which will send him to his grave, and it is this which increases the tragic irony of the scene. What we have, then, in this passage is a conflict between what Esther (as the narrator) thinks she is telling the reader, and what the reader understands from the scene, and from how it is presented. Esther, as a character, and Dickens, as a narrator, are both desperate to discover order in the scene, but the details of the scene defy them both and the reader is left with a deep sense of the emotional chaos at the centre of Richard's character. This begins to take us into another area altogether: that of Dickens's role as narrator and the way in which he presents the novel's story. Indeed, in *Bleak House* much of the novel's interest results precisely from this interplay between the first- and third-person narrators and the way in which the reader accounts for and interprets the stories they tell. But, rather than consider these questions at the moment, it will be useful to stand back and take stock of how our interpretation of the novel has developed so far.

6   *Have I achieved a sufficiently complex sense of the novel?*

I am aware of much that I have missed out in this analysis of *Bleak House*. I have concentrated on identifying some of the major themes in the novel, and in particular on character and the character's response to his or her surroundings. This has gradually moved me on toward the question of Dickens's role as narrator and the way he puts his novel together, and I shall be considering this in some detail later. For the moment, however, I shall try to sum up some of the main points that I have been making about the novel's thematic concerns.

Having said that, the first point I want to make might seem to have more to do with Dickens's style than with the novel's thematic interests. This is the point I was making in the first passage I analysed in this chapter, and a point I return to throughout this book: Dickens is a comic novelist, his prose distinguished by a highly inventive and exuberant use of language. This is one of the things that makes him something other than a moralising narrator, and his novels something other than a straightforward indictment of society. In fact, such details of style are intimately related to the larger thematic concerns that the novels seek to explore; even in apparently throwaway comic situations and comic details we can still perceive the larger concerns of the novel as a whole.

One of the major points made by *Bleak House* has to do with the way in which characters may be gradually worn down and eventually killed by a corrupt and inhumane society and its structures. What this should suggest to you is that, again, the basic conflict in a Dickens novel is always to be found in the conflict between money and love, which in turn introduces that general sense we have in *Bleak House* of an opposition between chaos and order.

If you think about it, you will see that everything that has come out of my analysis so far centres around this basic conflict; the whole novel, and all its concerns, can be understood in the light of this basic opposition. It is money, for example, which is at the very centre of the novel – in the shape of the Chancery suit – and it is money which temporarily poisons Richard's love for Jarndyce, making his experience of the world so disturbed and chaotic that he eventually comes to distrust Jarndyce, and dies because of the influence of Chancery upon him. Jarndyce, however, never loses his simple love for and desire to help Richard, and Richard's love for Jarndyce eventually returns, although too late to save him from the pernicious and destructive effects of Chancery and the world of money upon his life.

What Dickens seems to be suggesting throughout the novel is that in a corrupt and inhumane society many individuals will be both physically and spiritually destroyed. In such a situation individuals will always be the prey of an uncaring society from which they are powerless to escape. Some, like Lady Dedlock, will react against the civilised façade which society erects for itself by creating a façade of their own. But this can lead only to an inner, spiritual chaos in which life becomes meaningless and paralysed. A few, like Esther, will discover that the beauty and order to be found in the natural world may also be discovered in the self. But no truth and no beauty is ever to be discovered in a world defiled by corrupt social structures, such as the Court of Chancery. And running beneath all this there lurk the deeper, unfathomable impulses and desires which motivate and are a part of what it is to be human, such as Richard's desire to discover some meaning in life, or Mademoiselle Hortense's dark jealousies and ambitions which bring her to murder Tulkinghorn.

What you should remember is that, no matter how apparently diverse such thematic concerns may appear, they will always boil down to the basic conflict between money and love. The relationship between the many aspects of the novel will not always be immediately obvious, but, if you concentrate on the broad conflict between money and love to be found in any of Dickens's novels, and then narrow that down to the themes of the particular passage you are analysing, you will be able to see how the details of the text fit in to and illustrate something about the novel as a whole.

II   Aspects of the novel

The narrative structure of *Bleak House* is a particularly unusual and disturbing one: the narrative alternates with no apparent reason between Esther's limited first-person view of her world and the omniscient third-person description of the world at large. What the reader experiences is an apparently random collection of events and viewpoints which only slowly begin to cohere, since relationships between events which may be separated by several hundred pages are not immediately obvious. This means that the reader's response to the events can be managed to a nicety: the reader, for example, is given all the information from which to conclude that Lady Dedlock is Tulkinghorn's murderer, only to discover that she is in fact quite innocent.

Indeed, *Bleak House* is in one sense a type of mystery story revolving around the Chancery suit and its participants. What makes the novel something other than a whodunnit, however, is that the solving of the mystery is less important than the desire to solve it. There are three ideas which come out of this.

First, the Chancery suit, running straight through the centre of the novel, connecting everything and everybody to everything and everybody else, is clearly symbolic of life itself: the moment we are conceived we are, as it were, conceived into a suit of Chancery, which, like life itself, is a state of temporary permanence. Our experience of life always appears temporary, a succession of events waiting for that one event which will make everything permanent. Sadly, the only permanent condition we can expect is death, just as the Chancery suit can end only when it has ended Richard's life. Secondly, the fact that Dickens goes out of his way to present the world from different viewpoints suggests that the world cannot be understood from any single viewpoint, that its disorder is too complex to be seen from any single, fixed perspective. And, finally, the willingness of both the novel's characters and of the reader to engage in all manner of hypotheses to discover who did what, with whom, to whom and when, is indicative of the individual's desire to discover order even in the chaotic and apparently unconnected events described by the novel.

To follow some of the implications of these ideas and the narrative structure in which they are developed, it will be worthwhile to reconsider very briefly the passages I analysed in the previous section. Of the four passages I analysed, two were told by the third-person narrator and two by Esther. As you will recall, the two passages told by the third-person narrator went out of their way to create a sense of the world as chaotic, disordered, paralysed and without any consistent meaning or direction. In comparison, the two passages narrated by Esther portrayed a world in which meaning can be discovered; in Boythorn's garden, for example, Esther discovers a beauty in the natural world which is capable of being discovered within herself also. What this suggests is that, by giving parts of the novel to Esther, Dickens separates out two types of fiction. In the third-person sections of the novel he presents life as chaotic and disordered, whereas in the Esther sections he presents a much more purposeful and ordered view of the world in which things will turn out right in the end. Esther's misinterpretation of the state of Richard's soul in the last passage I analysed supports this view: Esther is so driven to find meaning and purpose in life that she wildly misinterprets the scene she is describing. The reader, noting this misinterpretation, sees in it a tragic irony also. What this suggests is that Dickens is playing with the notion of imposing fictional patterns upon the chaos of the world; in other words, he is setting the disorder of life (described by the third-person narrator) against the fantasy order of art (which is what we find in Esther's narrative).

We can see this most obviously in the fact that Esther is such an idealised, unconvincing, unrealistic and sugary-sweet narrator:

> They said I was so gentle; but I am sure *they* were! I often thought of the resolution I had made on my birthday, to try to be industrious, contented and true-hearted, and to do some good to some one, and win some love if I could; and indeed, indeed, I felt almost ashamed to have done so little and have won so much. (p. 73)

Esther's diffident honesty and devotion to others makes her an ideal of Victorian domesticity. But ideals aren't real, and neither is Esther. Esther's story is like her interpretation of Richard's state of mind: a falsification. If society is as chaotic and inhumane as the third-person narration suggests, then there is something highly suspicious about Esther's narrative progressing gleefully on toward a happy conclusion. But this, of course, does not negate the fact that, despite the crazy and destructive irrationality of the real world, we all of us search for meaning and some purpose in our experience of life.

Indeed, this desire to discover meaning and order, which is

often hidden in cryptic signs and clues, is at the centre of the novel. But this desire can be destructive also: Richard is destroyed both physically and emotionally by his obsession with the Jarndyce suit, which, in ending, ends him also. Krook, in his foul rag-and-bone shop where all the detritus of Chancery is stored, spends his time sifting through evidence he can neither read nor understand, scrawling letters in chalk on the wall and immediately rubbing them out before anyone else can read and discover the truth which they may hold. It is perhaps on the recognition of that truth that he spontaneously combusts, leaving old Smallweed and his family to discover the will which leads to the settlement of Jarndyce and Jarndyce. The following passage describes the scene at Krook's shop after his death:

> Regularly, every morning at eight, is the elder Mr Smallweed brought down to the corner and carried in, accompanied by Mrs Smallweed, Judy, and Bart; and regularly, all day, do they all remain there until nine at night, solaced by gipsy dinners, not abundant in quantity, from the cook's shop; rummaging and searching, digging, delving, and diving among the treasures of the late lamented. What those treasures are, they keep so secret, that the court is maddened. In its delirium it imagines guineas pouring out of tea-pots, crown-pieces overflowing punch-bowls, old chairs and mattresses stuffed with Bank of England notes ...
> The shutters are more or less closed all over the house, and the ground-floor is sufficiently dark to require candles. Introduced into the back shop by Mr Smallweed the younger, they [Weevle and Guppy], fresh from the sun-light, can at first see nothing save darkness and shadows; but they gradually discern the elder Mr Smallweed, seated in his chair upon the brink of a well or grave of waste-paper; the virtuous Judy groping therein, like a female sexton; and Mrs Smallweed on the level ground in the vicinity, snowed up in a heap of paper fragments, print, and manuscript, which would appear to be the accumulated compliments that have been sent flying at her in the course of the day. The whole party, Small included, are blackened with dust and dirt, and present a fiendish appearance not relieved by the general aspect of the room. There is more litter and lumber in it than of old, and it is dirtier if possible; likewise, it is ghostly with traces of its old inhabitant, and even with his chalked writing on the wall. (pp. 614–15)

The scene presented here is not only chaotic but also unearthly. Smallweed and his family lurk, 'fiendish', in the 'darkness and shadows', with old Mr Smallweed 'seated in his chair upon the brink of a well or grave of waste-paper' and Judy transformed into 'a sexton', groping about in the 'ghostly' room. The language used to describe the scene is the language of death and paralysis, and it is a paralysis which traps all of the characters involved with

Chancery. The Smallweeds can be found 'rummaging and searching, digging, delving, and diving among the treasures of the late lamented', just as many other characters in the novel spend much of their time attempting to put their various scraps of knowledge together to make sense of the world.

But on no occasion is all this energy expended other than for the purpose of providing power over another person. In the above passage, this power is directly linked not only with death but with money also: 'guineas pouring out of tea-pots, crown-pieces overflowing punch-bowls, old chairs and mattresses stuffed with Bank of England notes', and old Smallweed himself tries to extort money from Sir Leicester in exchange for Lady Dedlock's letters to the (significantly) dead Captain Hawdon. What is interesting is that these attempts to gain power and money are always frustrated by a perversity in nature itself, the perversity of death, which puts a permanent end to the temporary power provided by money. Tulkinghorn, for example, 'surrounded by a mysterious halo of family confidences' (p. 58), dies before he is able to make use of what he knows about Lady Dedlock. Even Bucket, who, as his name implies, is another depositary of human secrets, dipping down into the primaeval slime of the hidden and irrational, is unable to stop Lady Dedlock, who dies on the steps of the burying-ground.

In fact, Lady Dedlock's return to the burying-ground is indicative of a return to the formlessness of the fog with which the novel opens, and in which, as in the above passage, we can see 'nothing save darkness and shadows'. The physical world is as defiled by the fog as the inner, spiritual world is defiled and corrupted by the dirt and darkness of an inhumane society. Such a world encourages the very greed and self-interest which is most destructive of the purer instincts in humanity, making it difficult any longer to find a fixed moral centre to hold on to: the proselytising Reverend Chadband is a humbug and a hypocrite who joins with Smallweed in an abortive blackmail attempt. Even the basic principle of the family unit has broken down: Mrs Jellyby's children drag themselves up amidst dirt and neglect; Jo, the crossing-sweeper, 'knows nuthink' about his parents; Harold Skimpole turns his back on his responsibilities as a husband and a parent and lives a life of self-delusion, self-interestedness and selfishness, sponging on his friends. Set against this decay we find another group of people, motivated by purer instincts, attempting to hold together something of the natural love that exists between people – people like Esther, Ada, Jarndyce, Sergeant George and Mr and Mrs Bagnet.

But the overall vision of the novel is a decidedly pessimistic one. Things may come out all right in the end, but, as we have seen, there is something very suspect about Esther's story and the version of reality she describes. The contrast between this and the highly pessimistic version of reality given us by the third-person narrator makes our response to the novel uneasy. This uneasiness is particularly evident when we consider the types of characters who inhabit the fictional world of *Bleak House* and when we consider the comic manner in which Dickens presents them to us. One such character is Harold Skimpole. The following passage comes from early in the novel, and introduces Skimpole to us for the first time:

When we went downstairs, we were presented to Mr Skimpole, who was standing before the fire, telling Richard how fond he used to be, in his school-time, of football. He was a little bright creature, with a rather large head; but a delicate face, and a sweet voice, and there was a perfect charm in him. All he said was so free from effort and spontaneous and was said with such a captivating gaiety, that it was fascinating to hear him talk. Being of a more slender figure than Mr Jarndyce, and having a richer complexion, with browner hair, he looked younger. Indeed, he had more the appearance in all respects, of a damaged young man, than a well-preserved elderly one. There was an easy negligence in his manner, and even in his dress (his hair carelessly disposed, and his neckerchief loose and flowing, as I have seen artists paint their own portraits), which I could not separate from the idea of a romantic youth who had undergone some unique process of depreciation. It struck me as being not at all like the manner or appearance of a man who had advanced in life, by the usual road of years, cares, and experiences.

I gathered from the conversation, that Mr Skimpole had been educated for the medical profession, and had once lived, in his professional capacity, in the household of a German prince .... And he told us, with great humour, that when he was wanted to bleed the prince, or physic any of his people, he was generally found lying on his back, in bed, reading the newspapers or making fancy-sketches in pencil, and couldn't come .... The prince, at last objecting to this ... the engagement terminated, and Mr Skimpole having (as he added with delightful gaiety) 'nothing to live upon but love, fell in love, and married, and surrounded himself with rosy cheeks'. His good friend Jarndyce and some other of his good friends then helped him, in quicker or slower succession, to several openings in life; but to no purpose .... Well! So he had got on in life, and here he was! He was very fond of reading the papers, very fond of making fancy-sketches with a pencil, very fond of nature, very fond of art. All he asked of society was, to let him live. *That* wasn't much. His wants were few. Give him the papers, conversation, music, mutton, coffee, landscape, fruit in the season, a few sheets of Bristol-board, and a little claret, and he asked no more. He was a mere child in the world, but he didn't cry for the moon. He said to the world, 'Go your several ways in peace! Wear red coats, blue coats, lawn sleeves, put pens behind your ears, wear aprons; go after glory, holiness, commerce, trade, any object you prefer; only – let Harold Skimpole live!'

(pp. 118–19)

What strikes me about this extract is how many quite contradictory sensations it creates in the reader each time it is read. At first, Skimpole seems a very attractive character, refreshingly innocent in a world which is otherwise so inhumane, unjust and cruel: 'he was a bright little creature, with ... a delicate face, and a sweet voice, and there was a perfect charm in him'. This type of childlike innocence initially seems to fit in well with the broader contrast in the novel between the natural simplicity of the human spirit and the greed and self-interest of the world of money. The result is that to begin with we locate Skimpole on the side of the good characters.

But, the more we find out about Skimpole, the less appealing he becomes. He certainly puts a great deal of emphasis on how he values love and friendship, on how he has no aspirations in the world and few material needs. But his view of the world is wholly self-centred. He has been trained as a doctor, yet preferred 'lying on his back, in bed, reading the newspapers or making fancy-sketches in pencil'. This contrasts very strongly with the devoted self-sacrifice we find in Allan Woodcourt later, for Skimpole turns his back on his responsibility as a doctor simply because he can't be bothered with it. Similarly, he allows other people to pay his bills and care for his children and turns his back on his moral responsibilities in the world simply because he can't be bothered with it: 'All he asked of society was, to let him live.'

This is the point at which we find him most unattractive. There is no doubt that Jo, the crossing-sweeper, and thousands of others like him, would want few of the elegancies of life Skimpole sees as fundamental to his material needs: 'His wants were few. Give him the papers, conversation, music, mutton, coffee, landscape, fruit in the season, a few sheets of Bristol-board, and a little claret.' To make matters worse, Skimpole sees the German prince by whom he was employed to alleviate suffering, and the tradespeople who expect to be paid for the goods they supply, as mildly amusing, absurdly expecting him to fulfil his side of the bargain.

The emotions in the reader are fairly tangled by this time. On the one hand, we are impressed by Skimpole's intelligence, the wit and shrewdness of his logic and the stylistic mastery with which Dickens creates his character. But, on the other hand, we are disturbed by the fact that we do find this character so appealing. What this points to is the idea that if such characters can exist alongside characters such as Jo the crossing-sweeper, and if we, as readers, can find him amusing and interesting, then not only is life disordered and perverted, but our own view of the world is also disordered and perverted. We feel almost ashamed that characters like Skimpole can exist, but ashamed, too, that we can find him appealing. This is at the core of Dickens's comic technique. While creating a marvellously exuberant, intelligent and witty character, Dickens at the same time draws attention to the luxury of the position from which we can regard him and he can regard others: we end by feeling ashamed of ourselves for finding such a character at all appealing, yet enjoying the stylistic mastery by which his character is created.

The vice which characterises Harold Skimpole is selfishness, but it is a vice of which he appears wholly unaware, and of which he is only too willing to accuse others. In his memoirs published after his death, Skimpole writes of Jarndyce, 'Jarndyce, in common with most other men I have known, is the Incarnation of Selfishness' (p. 887). Self-delusion is always funny, in a tragi-comic way, and is a recurring feature of Dickens's comic figures. One thing about self-delusion is that it gives the reader a cosy sense of superiority over the character, since the reader sees the extent of the character's self-delusion while the character does not. But this sense of superiority brings with it an uneasy peace, because it is itself very close to superciliousness, and superciliousness is itself very close to self-delusion; the supercilious manner in which Skimpole dismisses the claims of the German prince and of the tradespeople to whom he owes money is itself very close to the way in which we dismiss Skimpole as a despicable character. Self-delusion is very close to our whole experience of Dickens's comic technique, and is perhaps a little too close to home for us always to find it reassuringly comic. Consequently, beneath Dickens's comic tone there is always a sense of uneasiness, and this is sharpened by our enjoyment of the stylistic virtuosity with which Dickens creates his characters and the world they inhabit.

One result of Dickens's comic technique, as I have suggested, is a certain sense of superciliousness in the characters, in the narrator, and consequently in the reader: Dickens's comic characters arrive, fully grown, explosively caricatured and unchanging. Consequently, these characters are denied many of the feelings which we associate with the human condition: for Guppy to profess his love for Esther is unpleasant, simply because Guppy is unpleasant and therefore incapable of any of the purer feelings which motivate humanity. All the purer feelings are best left to other characters, characters such as Jarndyce, Woodcourt and Richard. This may seem a crude way of stating things, and possibly reflects a crudity in the way Dickens's novels work, but it does mean that our experience of certain characters is made that much more memorable, since they are surrounded by unchanging aspects of humanity (such as greed, affectation and self-interest), against which their development can be measured.

Take the case of Richard, and his vampire-like legal attendant, Vholes. Vholes, picking at his pimples with his black-gloved hands, is a marvellous comic creation, and serves to tell us a great deal about the nature of Richard's gradual physical and emotional decline, and of his experience of life. Vholes becomes a physical embodiment of the obsession which is slowly destroying Richard: sitting in the coach, Vholes waits 'quite still, black-gloved, and buttoned-up, looking at him [Richard] as if he were looking at his prey and charming it' (p. 591); at the end of the Chancery suit, Vholes gives 'one gasp as if he had swallowed the last morsel of his client' (p. 924).

This metaphorical consuming of Richard by Vholes precisely parallels what happens to him: Richard is consumed by his obsession with the Chancery suit, just as the Chancery suit is itself consumed by its own costs. The function of Vholes here is to act as an unchanging and symbolic equivalent of the Chancery suit which destroys Richard, and this gives us a much greater awareness of the emotional reality of Richard as a character than would otherwise be the case. Beneath the surface of Vholes as a comic character we are being offered a picture of greed and a cruel lack of concern for other people. Again, we can see how a comic style of writing can simultaneously offer us a very dark and disturbing view of the world. Vholes and all the other comic characters may be lacking in any sense of human change or development, and they may at times seem too greatly caricatured, but it is against that unchanging backcloth of greed, self-interest, lust and affectation represented by these characters that we perceive the human reality with which Dickens's novels deal. Consequently, Richard can define his sensation of living permanently in a 'temporary condition' (p. 377), his hope lodged in the eventual settlement of the Chancery suit, but a settlement which, once reached, will devour him as greedily as Vholes devours both his client and his fortune. Richard finds no settlement in life because life, like the Chancery suit, is always temporary; waiting for some point at which things will be more settled is to wait only for death, and is, Dickens seems to be suggesting, what it is to be human.

Part of *Bleak House* has to do, then, with exploring the nature of the human condition in a cruel, unjust and inhumane society. What the novel demonstrates is that life is untidy, chaotic and disordered, and it stresses this by contrasting the purposefulness of the story told by Esther with the general chaos of the fog out of which the novel as a whole is born. This draws our attention to the formlessness of social existence and stresses the importance of personal relationships between people in a society in which there is no recognition of individual needs and feelings. Sadly, such human contact appears to occur to a great extent only in the story told by Esther – and that story is not necessarily a true representation of the nature of reality and of the human condition. Esther, as an ideal version of the Victorian ideal of domesticity is untrue to life, the human in the piece being Richard. But Richard is destroyed by the very system into which he is born, suffering all the hopes, fears, desires and thwarted ambitions of all of us. Esther's simple honesty, devotion and domesticity make her ideal. But ideals aren't flesh and blood human beings.

Such conclusions seem to represent a deeply pessimistic view of the world. And yet, beneath this pessimism, there is a barely hidden desire for order and an implicitly preferable alternative. On the one hand, the story of *Bleak House* ends with Lady Dedlock's death on the steps of the paupers' burying-ground, which seems to return us to the anonymous and all-pervasive fog which began the story. But, on the other hand, there is a deep sense of order and moral purpose in her death also. Her body is taken and entombed in the mausoleum within the grounds of Chesney Wold, alongside rows and rows of Sir Leicester's ancestors. This is the same respect for the past and for order as we find in Sir Leicester himself, and who, for much of the novel, has been a source of amusement both for the narrator and for the reader. But at the end of the novel we quite suddenly find ourselves respecting Sir Leicester and the sense of a moral fixity and purpose which he represents. If the choice is only between the formlessness of the fog and the obscurity of the paupers' burying-ground, Dickens seems to be suggesting, then there really is no hope for humanity. But he does find hope, and it is ironic that he finds it in Sir Leicester Dedlock, a character who has, for much of the novel, been the butt of his most savage irony. Humanity, and despite the formlessness of its social existence, seems to insist, just as Dickens insists with his ideal of Esther, to resolve things into some final hope. There is always something in the nature of humanity, and despite its show, its affectation, its self-interestedness, its greed and its envy, which is calling out for order, for a just, humane and morally stable society – even, for hope.

5

Martin Chuzzlewit

I Constructing an overall analysis

Martin Chuzzlewit is in some ways an easy novel to understand, because its major theme is so obviously stated throughout. Dickens even tells us, in his Preface to the novel, exactly what he has set out to do: 'to exhibit in a variety of aspects, the commonest of all the vices; to show how Selfishness propagates itself; and to what a grim giant it may grow' (Preface to the Cheap Edition, p. 39 in the Penguin edition, 1985).

Just because the novel's main theme does seem to be so clearly stated, however, does not mean we should approach this novel any differently. Remember that your analysis is only going to be worth anything if you can identify something of the distinctive quality of the novel. Just noting the theme of selfishness is not an adequate response.

So in this chapter I shall set about analysing *Martin Chuzzlewit* in exactly the same way as described in the previous chapters, except that, on this occasion, I am going to pay slightly more attention to Dickens's role as narrator and to the way he presents his work. As always, though, I start with the story.

1 *After reading the novel, think about the story and what kind of pattern you can see in the text*

Martin Chuzzlewit tells the story of Martin, the grandson of the irascible old Martin Chuzzlewit, a wealthy, elderly man who has become very suspicious of the selfish greed of members of his family. Young Martin, to spite his grandfather, gets himself apprenticed to another relative, the hypocritical Pecksniff. Learning of this, and seemingly taken in by Pecksniff's fawning, Martin's grandfather persuades Pecksniff to dismiss him. Young Martin determines to go to America with Mark Tapley, intent on making his fortune and returning to marry his grandfather's young guardian, Mary Graham. But while in America he is duped by the fraudulent Eden Land Corporation, loses all his money, and nearly dies of fever. Returning to England, he discovers his grandfather has moved in with Pecksniff, who is now trying to bully Mary Graham into marrying him so that he will benefit from the old man's will. But old Martin has not been taken in by Pecksniff and has been living with him only so that he can see at first hand the depths of Pecksniff's hypocrisy and meanness. Satisfied of the true nature of Pecksniff's character, the old man exposes him for what he is and unites the two young lovers, Mary and young Martin.

The incidents from which the novel springs are unusual. Mary and Martin have fallen in love before the novel opens, and old Martin's suspicions about the greed and selfishness of the members of his family are to a large extent based upon events we haven't seen. This tells us a good deal about the novel, for, although at a first glance the novel is quite clearly another novel about a young man maturing, its major interest has to do with something rather more abstract: the way in which people are suspicious of each other's motives. If we now think about this idea a little more, we can see a familiar pattern emerging.

The first thing to notice is that Mary and young Martin have fallen in love. Next, that old Martin suspects his family of selfish motives. The reason why he suspects his family of selfish motives is that he believes they are all hoping to benefit from his will when he dies. On the one hand, we have what we presume to be a simple and natural love between Mary and young Martin; on the other, we have old Martin's suspicions that his family love his money more than they love him. As in all Dickens's novels, then, we find the familiar conflict between money and love, and it is this which gives rise to old Martin's suspicions of his family's selfishness and greed.

This basic conflict between money and love is expressed in the story by another opposition: the opposition between the old and the new. Martin has to leave the old country of his home and go to the new country (America) to learn the lesson of unselfishness. Much the same holds true for the other characters in the novel, who also have to leave their homes to find out what their place in the world really is, but it is in the character of old Martin that the parallel is most obvious.

Old Martin is a mirror-image of young Martin: both start the novel as selfish, both go through a learning-process, and both have lost their selfishness by the end of the novel. But one is young Martin, the other is old Martin. Because the theme of selfishness is repeated in both young and old Martin, this suggests that what Dickens is talking about is the *recurrence* of human failings and weaknesses. This idea is supported by the fact that it is in the new country that young Martin is swindled: there is no clean divide between new and old whereby new is wholly good and the old wholly bad, or *vice versa*. Consequently, the novel is less an indictment of new sharp practices than it is an analysis of the perennial weaknesses of humanity.

One final point can be made about the story. That is its creakiness. The story is very obviously full of parallels and coincidences, shared names, biblical references, and so on. It also goes out of its way to make sure that young Martin and Mary are finally reunited, and to bring all its characters together at the end of the story, thereby implying that all the good characters will live happily ever after. *Martin Chuzzlewit* is a story which is very much more like other stories than it is like life, and this suggests that in this novel Dickens is more intent on entertaining and on producing a literary performance than he is on presenting any really profound analysis. Indeed, it is Dickens's fine comic performance and invention which give the novel as a whole its distinctive quality. We can see this in the style of the opening.

2   *Analyse the opening paragraph or two of the novel and try to build on the ideas you have established so far*

As no lady or gentleman, with any claims to polite breeding, can possibly sympathise with the Chuzzlewit Family without being first assured of the extreme antiquity of the race, it is a great satisfaction to know that it undoubtedly descended in a direct line from Adam and Eve; and was, in the very earliest times, closely connected with the agricultural interest. If it should ever be urged by grudging and malicious persons, that a Chuzzlewit, in any period of the family history, displayed an overweening amount of pride, surely the weakness will be considered not only pardonable but laudable, when the immense superiority of the house to the rest of mankind, in respect of this its ancient origin, is taken into account.

It is remarkable that as there was, in the oldest family of which we have any record, a murderer and a vagabond, so we never fail to meet, in the records of all old families, with innumerable repetitions of the same phase of character. Indeed, it may be laid down as a general principle, that the more extended the ancestry, the greater the amount of violence and vagabondism: for in ancient days, those two amusements, combining a wholesome excitement with a promising means of repairing shattered fortunes, were at once the ennobling pursuit and the healthful recreation of the Quality of this land. (p. 51)

The central opposition in this passage can be found in the conflict between its apparent subject and its real subject. Apparently the passage is talking about the history of the Chuzzlewit family, but it does this in such an elaborate, inflated and pompous manner that the reader finds another significance in the narrative: the absurdity of social life. It is absurdly pretentious, for example, to liken the history of any family to the complete history of the human race, yet this is precisely what polite society appears to do: 'it is a great satisfaction to know that it undoubtedly descended in a direct line from Adam and Eve'. Similarly, and equally pretentious, is the claim made by polite society that, just as all the 'best' families have some connection with the landed country gentry, so the Chuzzlewits have been 'from the very earliest times, closely connected with the agricultural interest'. Clearly, the tone of the passage is exuberantly ironic: we are not meant to take all this as a serious description of the history of the Chuzzlewits, but are rather meant to take it as a comment on the absurdity of social pretensions.

What this means is that the passage is finding another way to talk about things which are really quite distasteful. The family's murderers and vagabonds, for example, are justified on the basis that, if Cain is a part of the oldest recorded family, then it is of course quite right and natural that the Chuzzlewits (being equally ancient) will have their own murderers and vagabonds. This is precisely the type of logic which allows society to fool itself into a belief in its own 'polite breeding' and its own pretensions. To put it bluntly, society (like the passage) finds another way of talking about things, a way of pretending that the most barbaric acts (such as murder) or the worst excesses of an 'overweening family pride' can be made socially agreeable, and, indeed, 'not only pardonable but laudable'. The difference is that, while polite society absurdly believes in its own pretensions, the tone of the passage, by keeping itself aloof, distanced and ironic, can hold the pretensions of 'polite' society up for ridicule.

Even in this aloof, comic and inflated introduction, however, there are still hints at the deeper, irrational impulses which make up human beings, impulses which society may be unable to control. Murder and vagabondism, pride and violence are all mentioned in the opening paragraphs of the novel, and actually form a large part of the novel's story. These aspects of human nature represent a threat to the notion of civilised, 'polite' behaviour, and society may be unable to control these darker passions. Perhaps, indeed, this is why society does find some other way of talking about them, and of reconciling them to itself: simply because these impulses are uncontrollable. To find some way of reconciling them to civilised behaviour does, in a way, allow some form of control over them, albeit of a limited kind.

This allows us to identify much of what the novel is about: not only the fact of vagabondism, of violence, murder and pride, but also the way in which society attempts to control what may ultimately be uncontrollable. Much of the novel, for example, has to do with the public front characters create to face the world: Mould, the undertaker, glances 'at himself in the little shaving-glass, that he might be sure his face had the right expression on it' (p. 387); Pecksniff, after he has inadvertently discovered that Mary has told Tom of his despicable hypocrisy and bullying, studies his face 'in the Parson's little glass that hung within the door' (p. 564), as if to be sure, before he faces Tom again, that he does not carry this hypocrisy on his face; Jonas, after murdering Tigg, is convinced that his guilt is 'written broadly in his face' (p. 805) and is consequently unwilling to meet anyone. This idea of creating a public image of oneself reinforces the notion that beneath that public face, beneath what other people see, there lurk dark, irrational impulses; just as, beneath the façade of society itself, there lurk barbarous, murderous and violent impulses.

No one character represents this division between the public image and the true essence of his character more obviously than Pecksniff, the arch hypocrite. Every action undertaken by Pecksniff is done with the aim of enhancing his public image, and this is ultimately extremely selfish. Pecksniff, for example, quite willingly marries Mercy off to the violent Jonas purely for the selfish economic advantages it may bring him in the long run.

Analysis of any passage featuring Pecksniff would provide a vivid illustration of his hypocrisy and selfishness. However, another of the characters who catches my attention in relation to this theme is Mrs Gamp, so for my next piece of analysis I want to find a passage in which she appears.

3 *Select a second passage for discussion*

It is impossible to read *Martin Chuzzlewit* without being left with a very powerful impression of the hilarious Sairey Gamp. With her ill-fitting pattens, her wild umbrella and her little bottle on the chimney-piece she is one of Dickens's most memorable characters. The following scene occurs after the death of Anthony Chuzzlewit, and involves old Chuffey, who is tormented by the knowledge that Jonas had attempted to murder his own father:

> No doubt with the view of carrying out the precepts she enforced, and 'bothering the old victim' in practice as well as in theory, Mrs Gamp took him [Chuffey] by the collar of his coat, and gave him some dozen or two of hearty shakes backward and forward in his chair; that exercise being considered by the disciples of the Prig school of nursing (who are very numerous among professional ladies) as exceedingly conducive to repose, and highly beneficial to the performance of the nervous functions. Its effect in this instance was to render the patient so giddy and addle-headed, that he could say nothing more; which Mrs Gamp regarded as the triumph of her art.
>
> 'There!' she said, loosening the old man's cravat, in consequence of his being rather black in the face, after this scientific treatment. 'Now, I hope you're easy in your mind. If you should turn at all faint, we can soon rewive you, sir, I promige you. Bite a person's thumbs, or turn their fingers the wrong way,' said Mrs Gamp, smiling with the consciousness of at once imparting pleasure and instruction to her auditors, 'and they comes to wonderful, Lord bless you!'
>
> As this excellent woman had been formally entrusted with the care of Mr Chuffey on a previous occasion, neither Mrs Jonas nor anybody else had the resolution to interfere directly with her mode of treatment: though all present (Tom Pinch and his sister especially) appeared to be disposed to differ from her views. For such is the rash boldness of the uninitiated, that they will frequently set up some monstrous abstract principle, such as humanity, or tenderness, or the like idle folly, in obstinate defiance of all precedent and usage, and will even venture to maintain the same against the persons who have made the precedents and established the usage, and who must therefore be the best and most impartial judges of the subject. (pp. 786–7)

The first thing we must notice about this passage is what a brilliant piece of writing and characterisation it is. Very few novelists could produce within so little space so much humour and such a strong sense of character. But there is much more to this passage even than this, for the presentation of Mrs Gamp reinforces several of the novel's central themes.

The extract is certainly comic. One of the things that makes it comic is the external stance of the narrator. The narrator seems to hold himself aloof from what he is reporting, so that we see what is in reality Mrs Gamp's straightforwardly inhumane treatment of old Chuffey. She is, for example, apparently unaware of the true nature of her nursing skills: just as she rearranges her patients' rooms (and her patients) for the ease of her personal comfort, so here she treats poor old Chuffey as a troublesome nuisance who needs to be quieted and rearranged. Having virtually asphyxiated the old man by her 'scientific treatment', he is so 'giddy and addle-headed' that he can say nothing more, and it is this – rather than his comfort – which Mrs Gamp regards as 'the triumph of her art'. Not the old man's peace of mind, nor the old man's comfort, but the fact that he is unable to trouble her any more by talking. It is Mrs Gamp's peace of mind and Mrs Gamp's comfort which are the aim of her treatment of old Chuffey. What is worth noticing here is that Dickens is not offering any particularly subtle insight into Mrs Gamp's psychology, but is presenting a simple idea, and making it effective through the delight with which he creates her character and behaviour.

This is reinforced by some marvellous touches. Mrs Gamp, apparently reassuring old Chuffey and the onlookers that he is safe in her hands, tells the assembled company of her means of revival: 'Bite a person's thumbs, or turn their fingers the wrong way ... and they comes to, wonderful ....' What is apparently intended to be some solace to the old man soon begins to sound more like a threat of physical violence than the application of nursing-care. And again, as in the opening passage to the novel, the narrator's stance is underpinned by a fine irony: 'For such is the rash boldness of the uninitiated, that they will frequently set up some monstrous principle, such as humanity, or tenderness ... in obstinate defiance of all precedent and usage ....'

The effect of this style of presentation is that it points to a darker side to the world Dickens is describing. Mrs Gamp, as we have seen, is wholly unconscious of the inhumanity of her treatment of the old man. Further, the protests of Tom Pinch and his sister are completely ignored. What this suggests is a frightening sense of the selfishness, the threat of violence and the general lack of concern for other people which are prevalent in society as a whole, and the inability of people like Tom Pinch and his sister ever to change things. Those who might complain of the cruelty of Mrs Gamp's treatment of Chuffey are brow-beaten by the very people who 'have made the precedents and established the usage, and who must therefore be the best and most impartial judges of the subject'. The passage is able to imply all this by presenting the situation and the character of Mrs Gamp in an ostentatiously comic way. Although we laugh at the visible surface which is presented, the uneasiness of the situation and the narrator's ironic stance allow the novel to tease out the deeper instincts that govern the individual and society at large. Mrs Gamp's behaviour, then, far from being the idiosyncratic behaviour of an idiosyncratic old woman, tells us about the wider issues of the novel as a whole.

But, if society is as cruel and unjust as this passage suggests, and if people like Tom Pinch and his sister are ultimately unable to do anything to change things, then this represents a very gloomy view of the world. Yet this particular way of looking at the world is created out of a fine piece of comic observation of details. Looking elsewhere in the novel, we find Dickens using this same interest in detail to create a rapid panorama of his world, as in the following extract, which describes Tom Pinch walking by the Thames early in the morning.

4   *Select a third passage for analysis*

There they lay, alongside of each other; hard and fast for ever, to all appearance, but designing to get out somehow, and quite confident of doing it; and in that faith shoals of passengers, and heaps of luggage, were proceeding hurriedly on board. Little steam-boats dashed up and down the stream incessantly. Tiers upon tiers of vessels, scores of masts, labyrinths of tackle, idle sails, splashing oars, gliding row-boats, lumbering barges; sunken piles, with ugly lodgings for the water-rat within their mud-coloured nooks; church steeples, warehouses, house-roofs, arches, bridges, men and women, children, casks, cranes, boxes, horses, coaches, idlers, and hard-labourers: there they were, all jumbled up together, any summer morning, far beyond Tom's power of separation.   (p. 697)

It is the speed of this passage in building up a panorama which first strikes the reader. Things appear to pile up one upon another to such an extent that any sense of coherence is lost. Consequently, the major tension in the passage is that between the rapid accumulation of details and Tom's inability to make any real sense of it all.

First, we notice that the scene is made up of things, and things which appear to multiply of themselves: 'shoals of passengers', 'heaps of luggage', 'tiers upon tiers of vessels', 'scores of masts' and 'labyrinths of tackle'. It is as if the world has gone momentarily crazy, producing and reproducing itself on a night-marish scale.

This is reinforced by the amount of activity in the scene: the oars are 'splashing'; the row-boats 'gliding'; the barges 'lumbering'. Yet none of this activity seems in any way connected, since nothing seems to be moving for any purpose. Instead, activity and movement appear to take place quite arbitrarily and apparently at random. What this suggests is that the world is caught up in a ceaseless and aimless round of repetition, and this is underpinned by the narrator's almost frantic desire to list everything in the scene: 'church-steeples, warehouses, house-roofs, arches, bridges, men and women, children, casks, cranes, boxes, horses, coaches, idlers, and hard-labourers'. But part of the point made by the passage is that everything is 'all jumbled up together', with no immediately discernible purpose to it all, nor any discoverable relationship between one thing and another.

And yet much of our sanity depends on the belief that there is some coherence in the world, and some organising principle behind the world, no matter how mysterious that coherence and principle may be. In order to find some coherence in the world presented in the above passage, the narrator is driven to the extreme lengths of attempting to mention everything in the scene, as if to mention everything would be to rediscover the order which the visible world so manifestly lacks. But not everything is mentioned, simply because it is impossible to mention everything; no organising principle is discovered, simply because all the activity in the passage is isolated and unrelated to anything other than itself. And this is what gives the scene that final nightmarish sense, the sense that the world is simply too multitudinous and proliferates too quickly for the mind to make any sense of it. Consequently, the world becomes a jumble, 'far beyond Tom's power of separation'. The narrator, faced with a world apparently out of control, imitates that runaway sensation with the runaway description he offers of the world.

It is worth noting, too, that this instability in the world is imitated in the instability of the narrative voice itself. Here, and throughout *Martin Chuzzlewit*, Dickens denies himself the comfort of a truly omniscient narrator. In this passage, for example, we have the sensation of sliding from the narrator's description of the scene to Tom's and back again, and this reinforces what the novel as a whole appears to suggest: that the world has no visibly coherent centre or organisation in which we discover meaning. There is no single, fixed perspective from which we can see things. Consequently, and because of the limitations of our perspective, we cannot expect to discover meaning in the visible world. Meaning, order and coherence are to be found only in the basic and simple love that exists between people, love such as exists between Tom and his sister. Removed from that, Dickens seems to be suggesting, the world is just as Tom discovers it here: a world of chaos, beyond our minds' power of correction.

This sense of chaos and disorder in the world is an affront to what started the novel: the beliefs of polite society. Indeed, *Martin Chuzzlewit* is full of events which affront the precepts of civilised 'polite' society: attempted patricide, blackmail, fraudulent dealing and murder all figure in the novel. Most of these are centred in the character of Jonas Chuzzlewit, so it will be interesting now to consider a passage featuring that character, to see how the presentation of his character fits in with what we have discovered so far.

5   *Select a fourth passage for analysis*

This is the description of Tigg's murder:

> As the sunlight died away, and evening fell upon the wood, he [Tigg] entered it. Moving here and there a bramble or a drooping bough which stretched across his path, he slowly disappeared. At intervals a narrow opening showed him passing on, or the sharp cracking of some tender branch denoted where he went: then he was seen or heard no more.
>
> Never more beheld by mortal eye or heard by mortal ear: one man excepted. That man, [Jonas] parting the leaves and branches on the other side, near where the path emerged again, came leaping out soon afterwards.
>
> What had he left within the wood, that he sprang out of it, as if it were a Hell!
>
> The body of a murdered man. In one thick solitary spot, it lay among the last year's leaves of oak and beech, just as it had fallen headlong down. Sopping and soaking in among the leaves that formed its pillow; oozing down into the boggy ground, as if to cover itself from human sight; forcing its way between and through the curling leaves, as if those senseless things rejected and foreswore it, and were coiled up in abhorrence; went a dark, dark stain that dyed and scented the whole summer night from earth to Heaven.
>
> (p. 802)

There is a very clear and straightforward opposition in this passage between the natural growth and decay of the trees in the wood and

the violent ending of Tigg's life. The end of the day comes naturally to the wood as the sunlight 'died away' and 'evening fell',
while Tigg has fallen dead like a lopped tree: 'just as it had fallen
headlong down'. What this indicates is a pattern in which the
human becomes inanimate and the inanimate becomes human.
Tigg's body, for example, is described by the pronoun 'it', while
the dead leaves are personified, apparently capable of feelings and
action.

But this is no straightforward personification of the leaves, in
which the leaves take on merely human-like characteristics, for
they adopt human values also: the leaves appear to 'reject' and
'foreswear' Tigg's body, apparently recoiling from it 'in abhor-
rence'. Likewise, Tigg's inanimate body, now dead and returning
to the earth, 'sopping and soaking in among the leaves', appears
similarly ashamed of itself, apparently attempting 'to cover itself
from human sight'. It is almost as if the people in the scene, one a
murderer, the other a blackmailer and fraud, have transgressed so
far from human, civilised behaviour that they have become incapable of their own humanity and have consequently taken on the
characteristics of the inanimate. Similarly, it seems that the
inanimate objects have absorbed human values to the extent that
they not only become like humans, but actually behave as humans
should. The leaves appear to feel what the reader feels, and what
the characters should feel but are incapable of feeling. In making
this type of inversion in which the inanimate takes on not only the
characteristics but also the values and emotions of the human
being, the scene provides a vivid illustration of the darkest motives
and actions intruding into and disrupting the order of the natural
world.

This is clearly a very difficult thing for the narrator to keep a
hold on. Here, for example, we seem to have an omniscient
narrator who knows in advance what will happen: that Tigg will be
murdered by Jonas and will never be seen again. But when it
comes to the point of the murder the narrator is forced to speak
directly to the reader, almost as if to make the reader partially
involved in the discovery: 'what had he left within the wood, that
he sprang out of it as if it were a Hell!' From this point on, the
narrator sees what anyone there could see: 'In one thick solitary
spot, it lay among the last year's leaves ....' Even in this secluded
spot, the events of the world are public: what is seen could be seen
by any observer, the reader included.

The effect of this is to stress that this particular action (the murder of Tigg) is not just particular, but universal also, linking the whole of society and humanity together; Tigg's blood, sinking into the earth, 'dyed and scented the whole summer night from earth to Heaven'. The particular action takes on a wider, social and even universal significance.

This passage, then, is one that again describes how the darker impulses which motivate human beings intrude into the natural and social order. In the end, Dickens seems to suggest that the tension between the simple love people should feel for their fellow humans and the dangerous greed and self-interestedness that motivate events such as Tigg's murder simply cannot be resolved. Jonas murders Tigg because of his own greed and self-interestedness, and to escape from the greed and self-interestedness which motivate Tigg to blackmail him. In this cyclic pattern, one person feeds off another, bringing about their mutual destruction, and there seems to be no way in which the values of the conventional world can be reconciled with the destructive anti-social behaviour of people like Tigg and Jonas.

6 Have I achieved a sufficiently complex sense of the novel?

I am aware of much that I have missed out in this analysis of *Martin Chuzzlewit*. I have concentrated on Dickens's approach as a narrator, and have therefore not said very much about the characters in the novel. I hope, however, that you can see how to tackle issues of content and character in the novel by applying the kind of approach that I have described in the earlier chapters: your focus would most probably be on how various characters fit into the basic conflict in a Dickens novel between money and love, asking what the character's relationship is to other characters, in the context of that basic opposition.

One thing I want you to remember, however, is that what we have discovered about Dickens's narrative method will always be just as significant in relation to his other novels as it is to *Martin Chuzzlewit*. From what we have seen in the above passages, the first thing we can say about Dickens's narrative technique is that, to a very great extent, he employs an external, comic approach. This means that rather than stepping in to point to the significance of the events he is presenting, Dickens's narrator describes characters and events in an exuberantly ironic, comic and external manner which allows all the slightly absurd traits in human behaviour to be exaggerated, and consequently recognised by the reader. The narrator exaggerates events and characters in an inflated, pompous and ironic description, and we, as readers, are asked to interpret what we see. This is one of the things that makes him something other than a moralising narrator. What is also important in this respect is the way in which this exuberantly ironic tone creates a narrator who is always a little aloof and distanced from the characters and situations he is describing. It is this which allows Dickens to create that sense of a nightmarish world with words piling up on top of each other to the extent that they appear almost to take on a physical and aggressive quality of their own.

All of these features of Dickens's manner of writing are attractive and appealing, but perhaps the most important feature of his method for those of us trying to write about his novels is the way in which all the details in the novels imply so much. In any passage we are likely to encounter images of the confusion and chaos of the world conflicting with images of the simple love and tenderness which can exist between people. But what is perhaps most distinctive about Dickens's style is the way in which the small details he employs constantly imply all the larger concerns of the novel and point off in all kinds of directions. In that last passage we looked at, for example, suddenly to invert the animate and the inanimate, just at the point when Tigg is being murdered, and so made inanimate, is a marvellously inventive way of raising again the larger concerns of the novel. In a world in which human beings appear drained of their humanity, Dickens transfers the feelings to insensate things, and this reinforces the narrator's presentation of a world which is made both formless and chaotic by the domination of the spiritual world by the economic and material. It is this idea that human beings have somehow lost control of a world in which *things* predominate that I want to explore in the next section, since this can tell us a great deal about the narrator's relationship to the world he describes.

II   Aspects of the novel

In this section, I want to push the ideas I have established so far a little further in order to identify the unique and distinctive quality of Dickens's narrative method in *Martin Chuzzlewit*. Broadly speaking, the narrator has told us of a world devoid of love and motivated instead by greed, affectation, selfishness and money. This implies an alternative in which the value of a simple and natural love between human beings may redeem the social world and the individual's relation to it. It is the way in which the narrator presents this idea that I want to explore in this section.

One thing I am particularly conscious of, however, is that so far I have said nothing at all about the American scenes in *Martin Chuzzlewit*. All too often, students seem to be at a total loss about how to deal with the American interval, simply because it does seem so very odd, and even unrelated to the rest of the novel.

Before we start on the analysis of a passage from the American scenes, however, it will be useful to spend a little time thinking about how this removal to another country functions in the novel generally. First, in the nineteenth century the idea of America as the Land of Promise, and a land in which the individual might escape from the class-ridden inequalities of Europe, was an extremely powerful one. Throughout the nineteenth century, hundreds of thousands of people emigrated to America, hoping to find a new world of freedom and equality. In reality, they often discovered the starvation, disease and degradation they had thought they were leaving behind them.

The next thing to remember about this removal to America is that it allows us to see a country and its institutions in the making. This not only allows Dickens to take a sideways swipe at the hypocrisy and affectation of the visited land, but allows us to see the hypocrisy and affectation of the society from which the characters have come, which functions as a type of mirror-image of the visited land. What this means is that many of the novel's ideas about society will be very clearly stated in these scenes in America, since we are seeing society's weaknesses in their plainest state. This does mean also that the American scenes are going to lack much of the subtlety of situation and character that we find in the scenes set in England and it is for this reason that many critics have complained of the weakness of the American interlude in *Martin Chuzzlewit*.

However, if we understand how this removal to America functions in the novel, we can avoid being led into that particular critical cul-de-sac. Baldly stated, the removal to America allows many of the novel's basic themes and interests to be very plainly stated, with America and England functioning as mirror-reflections of each other. So if you are still unsure about the novel's ideas about society, some further close reading of the whole American expedition could be extremely beneficial to you.

But I do not want to work through a whole series of extracts from the American scenes here. All I want to do is to look at one passage to see how it adds to our understanding of the novel as a whole. The passage I have chosen is a description of the land bought by Martin and Mark from the Eden Land Corporation:

> Their own land was mere forest. The trees had grown so thick and close that they shouldered one another out of their places, and the weakest, forced into shapes of strange distortion, languished like cripples. The best were stunted, from the pressure and the want of room; and frowzy underwood: not divisible into their separate kinds, but tangled all together in a heap; a jungle deep and dark, with neither earth nor water at its roots, but putrid matter, formed of the pulpy offal of the two, and of their own corruption. (p. 446)

The clearest opposition in this passage is the opposition between what we might expect to find in America and what we actually find. The land in which Martin had expected to make his fortune is a 'mere forest' which, by the end of the passage, has degenerated into a 'jungle deep and dark'. Furthermore, the passage seems to be returning us to some elemental form of existence, to the slime out of which existence grew. But this is no Eden, no earthly paradise. Rather, the slime out of which this existence grows is the slime of corruption, poisoning and stunting everything which grows out of it. The trees are 'forced into shapes of strange distortion', are 'like cripples' and 'stunted', feeding on nothing more wholesome than the 'putrid matter' of 'their own corruption'.

It does not take much of an imaginative leap to realise that this forest is itself representative of America and of human society as a whole. America, Dickens seems to be saying, or any land, is only as good as the moral nature of the people who inhabit it. This is underpinned by the fact that this description of the forest is strongly reminiscent of the city and its inhabitants we have left behind us in England: the trees are personified as humans who 'shouldered one another out of their places' as they might in the city; they are 'stunted', 'forced into shapes of strange distortion', and are in fact identical to the poor we encounter in Dickens's city underworld, who are similarly poisoned by the base motives and desires out of which they and their society come into existence.

This clearly relates to the rest of the novel. Here, for example, the trees, all fighting for existence in this crowded patch of slime, are 'not divisible into their separate kinds, but tangled all together in a heap'. This is reminiscent of Tom Pinch's sensation of things being 'all jumbled together' in the passage I looked at earlier, and is, indeed, exactly what we find in the novel as a whole: characters in *Martin Chuzzlewit* exist in a world which allows for no meaningful distinction between people.

If you think about it, the only thing which distinguishes one person from another in *Martin Chuzzlewit* is that one person has more money than another. This is why, for example, Tigg is unrecognisable as the monied Montague. But to measure everything, including people, on the basis of money, is to take away the idea of any unique, separate character. Each person becomes whatever money or possessions he has, and consequently, in the absolute sense, and like the trees in the forest, he becomes anonymous, incapable of being 'distinguished ... into separate kinds'. Consequently, the world evoked by this description of the forest is one that is not only reminiscent of the confused and entangled panorama of the city, but almost nightmarish in its refusal to divide and sub-divide itself into order. Instead, the world in which humans find themselves is 'tangled' and chaotic. What might redeem the world and make it a decent place in which to live is that always implied-alternative: love.

But there is very little love to be found in *Martin Chuzzlewit*, simply because the characters (with one or two exceptions) are all obsessed by their own selfish desires. This is nowhere more clear than in the character of Pecksniff, who, for the right financial inducement, could bring himself to love anything or anybody. In the following passage, Pecksniff ruminates on the changes appearing in the aging Martin, and on the honest virtue of his love for the old man:

> His [old Martin's] looks were much the same as ever, but his mind was singularly altered. It was not that this or that passion stood out in brighter or in dimmer hues; but that the colour of the whole man was faded. As one trait disappeared, no other trait sprung up to take its place. His senses dwindled too. He was less keen of sight; was deaf sometimes; took little notice of what passed before him; and would be profoundly taciturn for days together. The process of this alteration was so easy, that almost as soon as it began to be observed it was complete. But Mr Pecksniff saw it first, and having Anthony Chuzzlewit fresh in his recollection, saw in his brother Martin the same process of decay.
>
> To a gentleman of Mr Pecksniff's tenderness, this was a very mournful

sight. He could not but foresee the probability of his respected relative being made the victim of designing persons, and of his riches falling into worthless hands. It gave him so much pain that he resolved to secure the property to himself; to keep bad testamentary suitors at a distance; to wall up the old gentleman as it were, for his own use. By little and little, therefore, he began to try whether Mr Chuzzlewit gave any promise of becoming an instrument in his hands; and finding that he did, and indeed that he was very supple in his plastic fingers, he made it the business of his life – kind soul! – to establish an ascendancy over him: and every little test he durst apply meeting with a success beyond his hopes, he began to think he heard old Martin's cash already chinking in his own unworldly pockets.   (pp. 545–6)

This passage is quite clearly exuberantly ironic, describing Pecksniff in terms quite opposite to his real character: touched by the change in old Martin, Pecksniff, with his 'tenderness' and 'kind soul', makes it the business of his life to try and secure the old man's money for himself. What is particularly interesting in Pecksniff, however, is the extent to which he appears to fool himself. Throughout the novel there is always a sense of a certain 'self-convicting candour' (p. 777) in his behaviour, and this makes what would otherwise be merely distasteful humorous also. Again, however, Dickens is not offering any particularly subtle presentation of Pecksniff's hypocrisy here. What he does is to allow us to see from Pecksniff's perspective as well as reporting from the position of the omniscient narrator, so that we have the sense of seeing things from both the inside and the outside.

This conflict between an internal perspective and an external one is, in fact, signalled in the passage from the outset. The passage begins, 'His looks were much the same as ever, but his mind was singularly altered.' Immediately, the narrator draws our attention to Martin's external appearance ('His looks were much the same as ever'), and to the internal change that has taken place in him ('his mind was singularly altered'). The passage continues to stress this internal change in Martin: 'He was less keen of sight; was deaf sometimes; took little notice of what passed before him ....' Pecksniff interprets this as a process of physical and mental decay. What the passage suggests, however, is that Martin is looking inward upon himself, and discovering, of course, his own selfishness. This is why he appears to see nothing and to hear nothing – not because he is approaching senility, but because the trappings of the visible world mean nothing to his new awareness of his own inner nature. And this is why, too, that as 'one trait disappeared, no other sprung up to take its place'. What has identified Martin's character in the novel so far is selfishness, and as he comes to understand his own inner nature so this selfishness is lost. Pecksniff sees no other trait because he can see only the selfishness of which he is the living example. Nothing else appears to surface because Pecksniff couldn't recognise it if it did.

This is not to suggest, of course, that Dickens is recommending some type of monastic withdrawal from the real world. Old Martin quite plainly is aware of what is happening around him, and of what is happening to his spiritual nature. And this is more the point that Dickens seems to be making here: that the individual comes to knowledge of himself only by becoming aware of his emotional, spiritual and moral relationship to the outside world. This means recognising the social world for what it is, and Dickens's external comic method is perhaps the most effective narrative method by which the affectation and pretension of the social world can be represented.

What this makes plain is that to Dickens the trappings of the visible world are all in part responsible for the disintegration of the moral and spiritual nature of the individual. Pecksniff, for example, obsessed with the face he presents to the world, is eventually hoist with his own petard: impressed by the ostentatious wealth of Montague Tigg, and convinced that he is about to inherit old Martin's wealth, he sinks his money into the fraudulent Anglo-Bengalee company, and loses the lot. But it is precisely because he is himself obsessed by appearance and the way things seem to be that he can be taken in by the apparent prosperity of Tigg's fake company. Pecksniff's inability to see behind the façade of social existence is at the centre of the above passage, and is a theme at the centre of the novel as a whole.

This takes us again to the darker side of Dickens's view of the world, for what is implicit in all this is a frightening sense of the pretence and greed prevalent in society, and the rareness of any character motivated by goodness. The above passage, and the novel as a whole, points to the falsity of social behaviour, and to the mean, sordid and depraved motives underlying most people's actions. This is an extremely gloomy vision of the world, and one which apparently allows for little real hope for change.

And yet, in *Martin Chuzzlewit*, as in his novels generally, Dickens does have his little band of virtuous types: Mark Tapley, Mary Graham, Tom Pinch and his sister. And he has one or two converts, too, most notably the young and old Martins, who are changed precisely because of the conflict between greed on the one hand and goodness on the other. Young Martin, for example, finds in America a society motivated purely by self-delusion, greed and affectation, but is loved and nursed throughout his illness by the indefatigable Mark Tapley. Similarly, old Martin has on one side the greed, self-delusion and affectation of Pecksniff, and on the other the honest virtue and love of Mary Graham. These characters change because their hearts are taken by storm by the natural goodness and love of other characters, and they consequently learn to see themselves and the world from a quite different perspective.

But in a sense the idea of this little band of good characters is almost unsatisfying for the reader, and certainly out of step with the view of the world which the novel as a whole implies. These characters are quite simply too good to be true, and come across to the reader as merely constructed fictions of goodness. Yet this, of course, is exactly how they have to be, for, if the world really is as corrupt as Dickens seems to be suggesting, the idea that good people can change anything is itself only a fiction. A fictional ideal of goodness is thus set against the terrible reality of the depravity of the social world; we contrast how we would like people to be with how they really are.

This points to a basic conflict in the novel itself. At the end of the novel, for example, Dickens goes out of his way to pull everything together, even at the expense of any form of credibility. Chevy Slyme reappears as Jonas's arresting officer after an absence of several hundred pages; all the characters are drawn together under old Martin's directions to witness Pecksniff's final degradation; the hapless Bailey is literally brought back from the dead for a cameo appearance; even the poor couple who helped Mark and young Martin in America are miraculously transported the 5000 or so miles from Eden Valley to a street adjacent to Todgers's, where they are coincidentally discovered by a blissfully happy Mark Tapley. Clearly, any pretence of credibility is virtually destroyed by this violent reconnection of characters at the end of the novel, and there must be in most readers a fair degree of unease with the rapid coincidences which pull the novel to a close. It is almost as if, at the close of the novel, Dickens is finally unable to accept the implications of what he has been suggesting throughout his story: that the whole of social life is a chaotic and dehumanising charade in which good characters are always the losers.

But closing the novel off in this way does in fact fit in with much that we have discovered about the novel in our analysis. First, pulling all the characters together does stress the idea that the real world is a place of disorder and chaos, since it is only in art that such perfectly dovetailed coincidences as end the novel can ever occur. It is only in a story that events can be arranged in such an order, and the real world continues to frustrate our desire for pattern and order. Secondly, this tells us something of Dickens's larger motivation. It is as if Dickens, simply because he cannot find any real sense of order in the real world, sets against this a tidy fictional ideal of all the good characters finding each other, and the bad ones getting what they really deserve. But this is nothing more than a fictional ideal; in the real world, bad characters continue to flourish.

So, at the centre of *Martin Chuzzlewit*, what we find is a strong sense of the conflict between the disorder of life and the order of art. One thing we can notice about this is that we become, as readers, very aware of the fact that we are being told a story, and that the story is being consciously fashioned by the novelist. This is exactly the same type of narrative method as we noted in *Bleak House* earlier, and it is interesting that in that novel also we had the same pattern as we have found in *Martin Chuzzlewit*: a broad panorama of greedy and grasping characters caught up in a corrupt social world, with a small group of good characters set against them. This pattern seems to reinforce the conflict between the disorder of life and the order of art, simply because the real world is so affected, sordid and inhumane, and it is only art that allows us to reconcile what we know of the real world with our sense of human decency. It is this same pattern, and many of its consequences, that is central in the next novel we look at, *Dombey and Son*.

6

Dombey and Son

I Constructing an overall analysis

THE MAIN IDEA in this book is that the best way to approach a Dickens novel, or indeed any novel, is to try to see a pattern in the work as a whole and then to look at a number of passages, interpreting them in the light of the pattern you have detected. It is the simplicity of this approach that is so helpful when we are dealing with a novel as long and complicated as *Dombey and Son*. The place to start, as always, is with some thoughts about the pattern you can see in the plot.

1   *After reading the novel, think about the story and what kind of pattern you can see in the text*

When the novel opens, Mr Dombey is a rich, proud merchant and the head of the shipping-company which bears his name: Dombey and Son. His wife has just given birth to a son, Paul, although she dies immediately after the birth, leaving her daughter, Florence, distraught and alone. Dombey neglects his daughter to an unnatural degree, centring all his hopes on Paul. Paul, however, is a frail, thoughtful child, and, being sent to Dr Blimber's Academy for educational 'forcing', he quickly sickens and dies, despite the loving care of his sister Florence. This intensifies Dombey's animosity towards his daughter, and, disapproving of her friendship with Walter Gay, a menial in his counting-house, he sends Gay to the West Indies. Gay is shipwrecked and believed drowned, and this again leaves Florence alone.

Dombey, however, quickly remarries. His second wife is the proud, haughty but penniless Edith Granger, who had been married at eighteen but is now a widow being hawked for sale to the highest bidder by her mother, Mrs Skewton. Edith is as proud as

Dombey, although for very different reasons, feeling herself humiliated by her mother's unashamed desire to marry her off for purely economic gain. The marriage is a disaster. Edith and Florence, however, are devoted to one another from the first time they meet and this further alienates both of them from Dombey, who, in his arrogant humiliation of his wife, causes her to run off with his deceitful and fawning manager, James Carker. They escape to France, but Edith fiercely refuses to become Carker's mistress. Dombey, obtaining information from old Mrs Brown, who had sold her own daughter Alice for sex to Carker many years previously, pursues the couple to France, where he confronts Carker at a country railway station. Carker panics and falls into the path of an approaching train, which kills him instantly.

Dombey has lost everything: he has been shamed in the eyes of society; his first wife is long dead; his son is dead; his daughter, driven away by his ill-treatment, has married Walter Gay, who has miraculously survived the shipwreck and returned; his second wife has eloped with his own manager, who has left the firm of Dombey and Son on the brink of ruin. The inevitable bankruptcy soon follows, due in large part to Dombey's arrogant refusal to redirect the firm's affairs, and he is thoroughly humbled. Returning to him, Florence saves him from suicide and he finds peace with her, having learnt that his daughter's natural love is worth far more than all the pride and material wealth he had previously held so dear.

With the plot of any novel, you need first to think how it presents the basic conflict at the centre of the writer's view of the world. This holds true for any novelist, whatever his or her concerns, but in the case of Dickens this basic conflict is the conflict between money and love. Certainly, such a conflict is in plain evidence here: Dombey, despite all his money, does not know how to love, and it is only after he has lost his money that he is able to return Florence's devoted affection. At the centre of this is the theme which binds the novel together: pride. It is Dombey's self-glorifying pride that causes suffering to Florence, and in another way, to Paul; and it is the same self-glorifying pride that attracts to him the equally proud and worthless characters of Major Bagstock and James Carker, who eventually desert him, and, in the case of Carker, assist in his destruction. Again, as in the previous novels I have looked at, Dickens is suggesting the capacity of money to poison human relationships, both in the family and in society at large.

There is just one other thing I want to mention before we leave the plot synopsis and move on to some close analysis of extracts from the text. This has to do with the position of women in the novel. Looking back over the plot summary I am struck by the number of women who are mistreated and abused by the two major male characters: Dombey and Carker.

The most obvious example of this is Florence, neglected and finally mistreated by Dombey. A similar, although less explicit case is that of Dombey's first wife, who seems to exist merely in order to provide him with a son; that done, there is little reason for her continued existence and she promptly dies, little grieved by Dombey. It is, for example, only *after* Paul's death that Dombey looks about him for another wife, and he finds this in Edith Granger. She, too, is portrayed as a mere utility: she is pretty, a useful bauble for Dombey to have about him, and has been hawked about in rich society by her mother since the death of her first husband. Edith's position is paralleled by that of Alice Brown, who was ruined by Carker some years previously. Throughout the novel, women are prostituted in one form or another, made the subject of financial transactions, and sold for money, rank and social status. What all this goes to emphasise is the potential cruelty towards its weaker members of a society motivated by money. Victorian women, particularly married women, had virtually no rights whatsoever concerning money, and it was not until the Married Women's Property Act of 1887 that they achieved anything like the economic freedom we all take for granted today. Consequently, in a society so motivated by money and greed, its weaker members (that is, those who possessed no money, such as women and children) were always a prey to the unscrupulous, the corrupt and the powerful, who could quite literally buy a person's subservience both physically and emotionally.

This prostitution theme, however, is not merely a historical footnote to *Dombey and Son,* nor is Dickens taking either a particularly reforming or didactic stance about the treatment of women in Victorian society. But the prostitution theme does tie in with the novel's broader thematic concerns, and serves to illustrate other aspects of the novel's interests. Essentially, this is part of the novel's presentation of the way in which money is used to trade on and manipulate those who possess no wealth, and hence no power.

Dombey's feckless decision to send Walter Gay off to Barbados, for example, causes a great deal of suffering on the part of Florence, Captain Cuttle and Sol Gills, just as Carker's using of Alice Brown ruins her life completely. The abuse of women and the feckless decisions of those who possess power are interrelated, and part of a much broader theme: the relationship between money and love, between the commercial and the humane.

What we can begin to see from all this is the enormous complexity of *Dombey and Son*, and the way in which the novel operates on many levels simultaneously, with all levels being interrelated. It strikes me, for example, that, when I look back over my synopsis and compare that with my *experience* of reading the novel, then I am immediately aware of huge gaps. The synopsis, despite the fact that a great deal can be gleaned from it about the novel as a whole, simply does not do justice to the novel's complexity of organisation and its presentation of character. That the basic themes of the novel are those I have outlined above is indisputable, but the novel presents those themes in a way which ultimately defies any attempt at an abstracted summary, because of its tight internal structure and the way in which every event and situation in the novel hangs on to and is a part of something else.

This in itself tells us a great deal about the novel. In *Dombey and Son* it is not enough merely to say that Dombey sends Walter off to the West Indies because he disapproves of his friendship with Florence. Similarly, Edith doesn't run off with Carker just because of Dombey's arrogant humiliation of her. And Dombey doesn't humiliate her just because he wants her to toe the line. The actions of the major characters are motivated by psychological impulses which we can understand when we read the novel, but which are impossible to categorise in any abstract way. This is because in *Dombey and Son* Dickens presents a dramatic situation involving several characters undergoing considerable inner conflict and torment. I shall go on later to discuss the way in which the novel creates this sense of an inner psychological conflict in its major characters. For the moment, I want to identify the novel's major themes by analysing specific passages from the text (page references relate to the Penguin edition, 1980).

2   *Analyse the opening paragraph or two of the novel and try to build on the ideas you have established so far*

> Dombey sat in the corner of the darkened room in the great armchair by the bedside, and Son lay tucked up warm in a little basket bedstead, carefully disposed on a low settee immediately in front of the fire and close to it, as if his constitution were analogous to that of a muffin, and it was essential to toast him brown while he was very new.
>
> Dombey was about eight-and-forty years of age. Son about eight-and-forty minutes. Dombey was rather bald, rather red, and though a handsome well-made man, too stern and pompous in appearance, to be prepossessing. Son was very bald, and very red, and though (of course) an undeniably fine infant, somewhat crushed and spotty in his general effect, as yet. On the brow of Dombey, Time and his brother Care had set some marks, as on a tree that was to come down in good time – remorseless twins they are for striding through their human forests, notching as they go – while the countenance of Son was crossed with a thousand little creases, which the same deceitful Time would take delight in smoothing out and wearing away with the flat part of his scythe, as a preparation of the surface for his deeper operations.
>
> Dombey, exulting in the long-looked-for event, jingled and jingled the heavy gold watch-chain that depended from below his trim blue coat, whereof the buttons sparkled phosphorescently in the feeble rays of the distant fire. Son, with his little fists curled up and clenched, seemed, in his feeble way, to be squaring at existence for having come upon him so unexpectedly.   (p. 49)

What first strikes me about this passage is very simple: the distance between the characters. Mr Dombey is in one part of the room, his son is in front of the fire, and Mrs Dombey's presence is not even hinted at, although, as later paragraphs reveal, and as we should expect, she is lying in bed in the same room. But there is a curious distance between the characters which is indicative from the very start of the isolation of people from one another in the novel.

Yet, if any emotional relationship or physical proximity is lacking in the passage, wealth is in clear evidence: Dombey, 'exulting in the long-looked-for event, jingled and jingled the heavy gold watch-chain', as if he were jingling cash in his pocket. This suggests that Paul, at least in Dombey's mind, is somehow equated with so many stocks and shares, a financial investment boding well for the future continuance of the great firm of Dombey and Son. There is, however, none of the natural love and affection for the new-born child that we might have expected to find in the father. Instead, Mr Dombey is 'too stern, and pompous in appearance, to be pre-possessing'. Quite clearly, any natural relationship of love is lacking in the passage, the characters being identified instead merely by their wealth or investment value.

This idea that characters – notably the baby Paul and the ignored Mrs Dombey – are merely utilities and consequently fit subjects for economic consideration is given further support by the curious description of Paul, who is in the process of being toasted like a muffin in front of the fire, almost as if he is being prepared for Mr Dombey to eat. This is, in fact, a recurrent motif in Dickens's novels. Pip, for example, in *Great Expectations,* attracts the cannibalistic interest of Magwitch on the marshes: ' "You young dog," said the man, licking his lips, "what fat cheeks you ha' got .... 'Darn me if I couldn't eat 'em" ' (p. 36). Instead, he terrifies Pip with the story of the young man whom he is with difficulty restraining from tearing out his heart and liver and con-suming those delicacies, tenderly roasted. Richard, in *Bleak House,* is fed upon by the vampire-like Vholes, who, at the close of the case of Jarndyce and Jarndyce, gives 'one gasp as if he had swallowed the last morsel of his client' (p. 924). Characters in Dickens's novels seem almost literally to be fed upon by other characters, and this is plainly true in the case of Paul, who is merely fuel to his father's pride and obsession with continuing the family business, accumulating wealth at compound interest into the distant future.

That Paul is marked out in this way is indicated by the fact that Time already has its eye on him, as if preparing him, just as Dombey is preparing him for his preordained future. The gold watch-chain, which is indicative of Dombey's wealth and of his commercial plans for the young child, also links Paul inexorably to Time: 'which the deceitful Time would take delight in smoothing out and wearing away with the flat part of his scythe, as a prepara-tion of the surface for his deeper operations'. What all this sug-gests is not only Dombey's excessive pride and his obsessive desire for the continuance of the family business, but also his inability to feel any natural affection for the child, who is instead merely a part of his great plan for the future: Time's 'deeper operations' are a parallel to Dombey's future plans.

Baldly stated, then, we can see that what we have here is what we find in the novel as a whole: the isolation bred by wealth, and the capacity of wealth to destroy any natural affection in human relations. But it is important to notice also that the description of the scene, of Mr Dombey, 'too stern and pompous ... to be pre-possessing', is not just the description of an external arrogance and pomposity, but also a hint at the deeper and largely hidden solitariness and isolation this arrogance and pomposity engender. To Mr Dombey, Paul is merely an object necessary to continue the family business; in what should be a touching scene of domestic love we find plenty of business and commercial considerations, but no evidence of a family, and certainly no evidence of love. From the very start of the novel people are alone, isolated by the pernicious effects of wealth upon the world of the emotions. As if to drive home the impossibility of Paul's finding any affection in the world, his mother dies very soon after his birth, and Mr Dombey is forced to employ a wet-nurse for the child. The following passage describes the interview between Mr Dombey and Polly Toodle, who has been recommended to him by Miss Tox.

3   *Select a second passage for discussion*

> 'Oh, of course,' said Mr Dombey. 'I desire to make it a question of wages, altogether. Now, Richards, if you nurse my bereaved child, I wish you to remember this always. You will receive a liberal stipend in return for the discharge of certain duties, in the performance of which, I wish you to see as little of your family as possible. When those duties cease to be required and rendered, and the stipend ceases to be paid, there is an end of all relations between us. Do you understand me?'
>
> Mrs Toodle seemed doubtful about it; and as to Toodle himself, he had evidently no doubt whatever, that he was all abroad.
>
> 'You have children of your own,' said Mr Dombey. 'It is not at all in this bargain that you need become attached to my child, or that my child need become attached to you. I don't expect or desire anything of the kind. Quite the reverse. When you go away from here, you will have concluded what is a mere matter of bargain and sale, hiring and letting: and will stay away. The child will cease to remember you; and you will cease, if you please, to remember the child.'
>
> Mrs Toodle, with a little more colour in her cheeks than she had before, said, 'she hoped she knew her place'.   (p. 68)

The central conflict in this passage is between Dombey, who is motivated by the practical necessity to provide food for his son, and Polly Toodle, who is a mother. Dombey tells Polly, 'It is not at all in this bargain that you need become attached to my child, or that my child need become attached to you.' Clearly, some kind of machine designed to supply the requisite amount of milk would suit the child's needs as Dombey perceives them.

Opposed to this view of a mother is Polly, who intimates –

without, of course, declaring it to her potential employer – that sustenance cannot be provided without love. Having been told by Dombey that 'When those duties cease to be required ... there is an end of all relations between us', Polly is 'doubtful about it', while her husband, a loving and lovable type in the Joe Gargery mould, is at a total loss and 'all abroad'. He simply cannot understand the proposition. The idea of a child without the love a mother can provide is beyond his understanding of the world, while to Dombey it is 'a mere matter of bargain and sale, hiring and letting'. Despite Dombey's edict that 'The child will cease to remember you; and you [Polly] will cease ... to remember the child', the Toodles cannot envisage a world without the natural tie between the child and its mother – even if, as here, the mother is a substitute one.

And yet the episode is concluded on the principle of money because the Toodles have to bow to its power. The Toodles need money to live, Paul needs sustenance to live; and in Dombey's mind the two things are equated. But life is more than mere sustenance. Polly, saying that 'she hoped she knew her place', acknowledges the money principle, acknowledges her position in the social hierarchy and agrees ultimately to provide her body for payment. As Dombey tells her: 'I desire to make it a question of wages, altogether.' This is prostitution of a most genteel kind, but it is prostitution all the same, and Dombey's attitude makes it wholly degrading to its object. Finally, though, the degraded Polly, reddening and 'with a little more colour in her cheeks than she had before', is forced to accept that Dombey is simply buying her body, and ultimately denying her emotional existence. In fact, Dombey virtually denies her existence altogether beyond that which he requires. His desire for her to be known as Richards, for example, is no mere whim, but proof that he has bought her and that she now has no individual rights at all – not even the right to her own name. What Polly represents is the natural tie between mother and child; what Dombey wants is the practical and necessary supply of sustenance for his child, which, he believes, can be purchased, just as anything else can be purchased. The whole episode is to Dombey simply 'a bargain'. Polly needs money, Dombey is able to pay; he remains heedless of his arrogant and degrading treatment of her.

This ties in with the prostitution theme I identified earlier. Throughout the novel there is a central distinction made between, as Susan Nipper puts it, 'giving consent when asked, and offering when unasked' (p. 230). This, indeed, is the principle of prostitution in the novel. Edith, for example, plays piano and sings *at Dombey's request* (pp. 470–1], just as she agrees to marry him merely because she does not have the economic freedom to refuse, even though she loathes him and everything he represents. At every stage of the novel characters are aware of selling themselves for the use of another person; even Carker finally rebels against Dombey because he has been 'bought and hired' (see p. 686) by him, just as Alice was in turn 'bought and hired' (see p. 849) by Carker. And it is precisely this Dickens is stressing in the above passage: the importance of human feelings and personal contact set against an inhumane society, in which there is no recognition made of individual needs and feelings. But Dombey's view of the world, as the novel goes on to demonstrate, is an almighty sham – a point reinforced here by the fact that all Dombey wants is an artificial mother for his son. Indeed, Dombey's whole world is one of falseness and artificiality; beneath it there is nothing, because such a view of the world, in denying the existence of any emotional relationship between people, is unable to make any recognition of individual needs and feelings.

The character who suffers most under this inhumane artificiality is Florence. She lives in a fine house, has all the comforts of a civilised lifestyle about her, and yet is lacking in that one essential to existence: love. The following passage describes her life at Dombey's house immediately following the death of her mother:

4   *Select a third passage for discussion*

When the funeral was over, Mr Dombey ordered the furniture to be covered up – perhaps to preserve it for the son with whom his plans were all associated – and the rooms to be ungarnished, saving such as he retained for himself on the ground floor. Accordingly, mysterious shapes were made of tables and chairs, heaped together in the middle of rooms, and covered over with great winding-sheets. Bell-handles, window-blinds, and looking glasses, being papered up in journals, daily and weekly, obtruded fragmentary accounts of deaths and dreadful murders. Every chandelier or lustre, muffled in holland, looked like a monstrous tear depending from the ceiling's eye. Odours, as from vaults and damp places, came out of the chimneys. The dead and buried lady was awful in a picture-frame of ghastly bandages. Every gust of wind that rose, brought eddying round the corner from the neighbouring mews, some fragments of the straw that had been strewn before the house when she was ill, mildewed remains of which were still cleaving to the neighbourhood; and these, being always drawn by some invisible attraction to the threshold of the dirty house to let immediately opposite, addressed a dismal eloquence to Mr Dombey's windows. (p. 75)

The conflict in this passage is between the domestic articles which make up the scene and how those are transformed into images of death. All the details of the passage are concerned with items of everyday life: tables and chairs, bell-handles, window-blinds, looking glasses. But these are transformed into frightening and 'mysterious shapes' suggestive of sadness and death rather than of the lives of which they should be a part. The furniture is described as 'covered over with great winding-sheets'; the chandelier looks like 'a monstrous tear'; strange odours from the chimneys are described as if emanating from 'vaults'; a painting of the recently buried Mrs Dombey surveys the scene as if from her grave, framed by a winding-sheet, 'awful in a picture-frame of ghastly bandages'.

The effect of this style of description is to create a very uneasy sense in the reader that things are wrong, that irrational and potentially violent passions lurk beneath this transforming of a home into a mausoleum; the looking-glasses, for example, are 'papered up in journals' telling 'fragmentary accounts of deaths and dreadful murders'. This intrusion of violence and crime into the details of domestic life turns what should be a home into a place of unknown terrors, strange and violent passions lurking just beneath the surface. But this, of course, is exactly what Dombey's house is like. Florence lives her life wholly neglected by her father, even, eventually, hated by him. The suggestion in the passage of perverted and distorted passions perfectly mirrors the type of home in which Florence lives.

The sense that we gain from this of Florence's life is made that much more strongly by the effect of the final sentence. It is in this same house opposite that Florence later watches (p. 319) various scenes of domestic happiness between a daughter of her own age and her widowed father. The contrast there is plain enough. Another contrast made in the reader's mind must be between this scene and the sunny warmth and happiness of Sol Gills's household.

There is considerable irony in the way Dickens engineers the comparison between Dombey's house and Gills's home. On the surface, Mr Dombey's household is a real family with father and children, while Sol Gills's household includes only the crazy old

Cap'n Cuttle and the orphaned Walter Gay. But of the two it is Walter who lives in a real home, surrounded by love, and Florence who is orphaned and alone. This, as Dickens later asserts, is the cruellest fate that can befall any child: 'not an orphan in the wide world can be so deserted as the child who is an outcast from a living parent's love' (p. 423). Beneath all this, of course, and motivating Dombey's perverted passions, is his excessive pride and hope for his son. The furniture is 'perhaps' covered up, as the narrator tells, us 'to preserve it for the son with whom his plans were all associated'. But this is preservation only. It is the equivalent to a dead body being kept in a mortuary awaiting burial, and the house, its furniture, Paul and ultimately all of Dombey's hope and pride are already dead, already, like the furniture, wrapped in a winding-sheet awaiting burial. What Dickens demonstrates here, in a marvellously controlled and evocative way, is that Dombey is incapable, unlike Sol Gills and Captain Cuttle, of creating any sense of a home because he is emotionally dead, and his house can only mirror that emotional deadness.

5   Select a fourth passage for discussion

The following passage occurs shortly after the death of Paul when Dombey, having been befriended by Major Bagstock, is about to leave London to take a holiday at Leamington. This is how the Major greets him:

'Dombey,' said the Major, 'I'm glad to see you. I'm proud to see you. There are not many men in Europe to whom J Bagstock would say that – for Josh is blunt. Sir: it's his nature – but Joey B is proud to see you, Dombey.'

'Major,' returned Mr Dombey, 'you are very obliging.'

'No, Sir,' said the Major, 'Devil a bit! That's not my character. If that had been Joe's character, Joe might have been, by this time, Lieutenant-General Sir Joseph Bagstock, KCB, and might have received you in very different quarters. You don't know old Joe yet, I find. But this occasion, being special, is a source of pride to me. By the Lord, Sir,' said the Major resolutely, 'it's an honour to me!'

Mr Dombey, in his estimation of himself and his money, felt that this was very true, and therefore did not dispute the point. But the instinctive recognition of such a truth by the Major, and his plain avowal of it, were very agreeable. It was a confirmation to Mr Dombey, if he had required any, of his not being mistaken in the Major. It was an assurance to him that his power extended beyond his own immediate sphere; and that the Major, as an officer and a gentleman, had a no less becoming sense of it, than the Beadle of the Royal Exchange. (p. 345)

What we first notice about this passage is what a brilliant piece of writing it is, and how it creates so much humour and tells us so much about character in such a short space. Bagstock is a pompous windbag of Pecksniffian proportions, and Dombey ludicrous in his complacent belief in the truth of what Bagstock says. This is, in fact, the central opposition in the passage: the conflict between Bagstock's apparently veracious self-deprecation and Dombey's complacency. What the reader sees, and the characters do not, however, is the ridiculous affectation in such posturing. But Dickens doesn't attempt to offer any particularly subtle insight into the psychology of his characters here; he merely takes a simple idea – Bagstock's false self-deprecation and Dombey's complacency – and makes it effective through the delight with which he imagines these pompous gestures.

It is important to notice, too, how Dickens creates the scene. In this scene (and this is true of Dickens's comic technique generally), he observes from a distance what society tacitly agrees to ignore. This external approach allows the characters to hang themselves, because it permits Dickens to exaggerate all the slightly absurd traits in human behaviour to such an extent that we cannot help but notice them. Bagstock, for example, falsely claiming that the honour of this meeting is all his and that he, of course, is of minor importance beside the grand Dombey is, in fact, always talking about himself. He refers continually to himself by various names which serve always to keep him at the centre of things: 'J Bagstock would say ... for Josh is blunt, Sir .... Joey B is proud to see you.' In fact, in his first speech in the above passage, he refers to himself in one way or another no less than six times.

Dickens's external comic approach also allows him to remain always a little aloof from the proceedings, able to comment with such biting accuracy on the falseness of the characters he portrays, as here: 'Mr Dombey, in his estimation of himself and his money, felt that this was very true, and therefore did not dispute the point.' This detached and external view allows Dickens not only to represent in an exaggerated form all the falsity of social affectation, but also to comment ironically on it. Essentially, Dickens refuses to accept the falsity of social conventions by which we all agree to put on some kind of act for each other. But Dickens does not merely cut through all the falsity of the real world, he also offers some kind of refuge from it. For, if the real world really is as corrupt and false as characters such as Bagstock and Dombey seem to testify, then it is necessary that we not only see that affectation but also have some way of controlling it; Dickens achieves this control through his humour.

This takes us back to consider more precisely how the above passage works in the context of the novel. At the centre of the passage is a strong sense of the artificiality of the characters, and implicitly of the society in which they live. Later, for example, Dombey, stating his ultimatum to Edith, informs her, 'there are appearances ... which must be maintained before the world' (p. 745). Similarly, after Edith his left him, he is haunted by 'What the world thinks of him, how it looks at him, what it sees in him, and what it says' (p. 809). What this suggests is that Dombey, living in a world of pretence, has existence only by virtue of a masquerade, and this in turn reinforces the essential isolation of characters in the novel. If society really is just a masquerade, then there really is nothing for characters to hold on to, no values they can any longer trust. After Dombey's bankruptcy, for example, the worthy Bagstock declares that he has been 'mightily abused' (p. 910) by Dombey, and deserts him. It is at this point that Dombey can begin to turn to the only value there is left: Florence's love.

6   Have I achieved a sufficiently complex sense of the novel?

Dombey and Son, it can be argued, examines, as all Dickens's novels do, a persistent tension between social affectation, greed and money, and the natural expression of love between characters. This theme is, however, developed in different ways in different novels, and in addition each individual reader will see and interpret the issues with an emphasis of his or her own. The whole point in building your own response from a number of passages is to try to define this distinctive impression you have of the novel you are studying, so that you really manage to sort out and articulate your response.

Looking back over my analysis so far, for example, I am struck that while in *Dombey and Son* the basic conflict is that between money and love, there is a much greater sense in this novel of the underlying motives which move people than there is some of the other novels I have looked at in this book. In *Dombey and Son* we not only see the external arrogance of such characters as Dombey but are aware also of an underlying, internal part of his character. Living in a world of pride and falsity, Dombey is isolated within himself and quite cut off from other people. This sense of an inner and largely hidden world is very carefully created and handled by Dickens, as in the following scene, when Mrs Chick suggests to Dombey that Paul should be sent to Mrs Pipchin's in Brighton, and that he might be accompanied by Florence:

> 'Supposing we should decide, on tomorrow's inquiries, to send Paul down to Brighton to this lady, who would go with him?' inquired Mr Dombey, after some reflection.
>
> 'I don't think you could send the child anywhere at present without Florence, my dear Paul,' returned his sister, hesitating. 'It's quite an infatuation with him. He's very young, you know, and has his fancies.'
>
> Mr Dombey turned his head away, and going slowly to the bookcase and unlocking it, brought back a book to read.
>
> 'Anybody else, Louisa?' he said, without looking up, and turning over the leaves. (p. 159)

What marks out the genius in this piece of writing is Dickens's control over the situation, his ability to let the gaps in the text convey information to the reader. This in turn gives us a strong sense of the internal workings of Mr Dombey's mind and of his emotional state. That his dislike of Florence is generally known is indicated by Mrs Chick 'hesitating' as she makes the proposal to him, and this is quite obviously presented.

But what is much more subtly done is the emotional conflict in Dombey himself. Considering the project, he 'turned his head away, and going slowly to the bookcase and unlocking it, brought back a book to read'. It is in this space in the text, in which Dombey attempts to avoid the implications of Mrs Chick's suggestion, that the reader is able to perceive something of the workings of Dombey's mind, his sense of severe frustration that he cannot come anywhere close to Paul in the way that Florence does. Consequently, the relationship she enjoys with Paul is not something he can derive any pleasure from, as a father normally does, since it will always be a standing reproach to him, pointing out his own failings. Indeed, this is precisely why he so dislikes Florence: in her simple, honest affection, she loves and is loved in return by those Dombey himself wants to respect him – Paul and, later, Edith. Part of his problem is that he demands from these characters what the world appears to give him: respect. But, as we have seen in the case of Bagstock, this respect is a sham, motivated only by self-interest and deceit. The way in which Dickens achieves this depth of characterisation is brilliantly done, showing us not only the external image of arrogance, but also something of the inner, psychological and emotional turmoil it occasions in the character.

We can see much the same kind of inner turmoil in Edith, and it is, in fact, the conflict between these two characters which dramatises and gives flesh to Dickens's exploration of the psychological turmoil created in characters by the pernicious effects of money. The following scene describes Edith walking through the Dombey mansion just before her marriage:

> Slowly and thoughtfully did Edith wander alone through the mansion of which she was so soon to be the lady: and little heed took she of all the elegance and splendour it began to display. The same indomitable haughtiness of soul, the same proud scorn expressed in eye and lip, the same fierce beauty, only tamed by a sense of its own little worth, and of the little worth of everything around it, went through the grand saloons and halls, that had got loose among the shady trees, and raged and rent themselves. The mimic roses on the walls and floors were set around with sharp thorns, that tore her breast; in every scrap of gold so dazzling to the eye, she saw some hateful atom of her purchase-money; the broad high mirrors showed her, at full length, a woman with a noble quality yet dwelling in her nature, who was too false to her better self, and too debased and lost, to save herself.   (p. 503)

Just as Florence's very existence stands as a continual reproach to Dombey and his failure to understand the nature of simple love, so Dombey and his wealth stand as a continual reproach to Edith. In the above passage, this is expressed in a basic opposition between the fake and the real, and it is this which torments Edith's inner self, making her aware of how she has allowed herself to be degraded by wealth and artificiality. The 'mimic roses', for example, are 'set around with sharp thorns, that tore her breast'; similarly, 'in every scrap of gold so dazzling to the eye, she saw some hateful atom of her purchase-money'. What Edith recognises here is the extent to which she has been sold to an artificial world by an artificial mother, so that, to her mind, she has become as worthless and artificial as it: 'a sense of its own little worth, and of the little worth of everything around it'. Again, we can see in this passage a subtle working-out of the inner turmoil of the character's mind, the emotional frustration which society creates in its inhabitants.

We are now beginning to understand why it was that the plot synopsis at the beginning of this chapter, although useful, seemed an inadequate reflection of the experience of reading the novel. In *Dombey and Son*, Dickens dramatises the inner, emotional world of his characters to an extent not common in the other novels I have considered. Characters are no longer seen from a purely external perspective, with just the occasional insight into their motives, but work, as it were, from the inside, out.

This is not to say that the same does not happen in Dickens's other novels, just that, in this novel, we are particularly aware of it. The subtlety by which he manages to create this sense of an inner turmoil, as in the previous passage, or the way in which the world equates with and accuses a character's very existence, as in the last passage, demonstrates Dickens's exceptional control over his material, and the genius of his writing. It may well be that the central themes of *Dombey and Son,* as I hope to have demonstrated, are fairly easily identifiable. But it is also the case, again as I hope to have demonstrated, that those themes are worked out in a very distinctive way, stretching the novel to its utmost in its creation of its fictional world. Indeed, it is my belief that *Dombey and Son* really does stretch the novel as a form almost to a point where it begins to break down. To take this idea a little further, I now want to spend some time considering how the novel is put together.

II Aspects of the novel

Dombey and Son could be discussed in all kinds of ways. You could examine more extracts, concentrating on the novel's development of its themes; you could concentrate on the way in which characters interact and the emotional conflicts between them; or you could think about what the novel has to say about social change and on the position of women in Victorian England. But something that strikes me about *Dombey and Son*, and what I want to concentrate on in this section, is how structured and patterned the novel is.

We have already seen how in other Dickens novels we are often very conscious of the fact that we are being told a story and that the novel seems to go out of its way to pattern itself in a meaningful way, even if this means stretching to the utmost the reader's ability to suspend belief. At the end of *Martin Chuzzlewit,* for example, Dickens goes to fantastic lengths to get all his good characters married off together and to promise future happiness for all the people who deserve it, even resurrecting young Bailey from the dead to make a final, if somewhat dizzy appearance. We find similar things happening at the end of *Dombey and Son*: the demented Bunsby is married, albeit unwillingly, to the redoubtable Mrs MacStinger; Toots to Susan Nipper; Towlinson to the housemaid with a predilection for foreigners with whiskers; Morfin to Miss Carker; Mr Feeder BA to Cornelia Blimber (in new spectacles); and, of course, Walter to Florence – good old Cap'n Cuttle escaping meanwhile in the slenderest terms from the attentions of a widow by the name of Bokum who would otherwise have had him married by force.

But there is much more to all this than merely Dickens's desire to pull all the strands of his story together at the end, for ending a novel in this way does in fact stress the disorder and chaos of the real world by comparison with the order and pattern of the world of art. This idea is at the centre of the novel: the emotional and psychological turmoil of such characters as Edith and Mr Dombey conflicts with the artificial front they put on for the world to see, and it is when this collapses – when Edith refuses to keep up appearances as Dombey's devoted wife – that the conflict reaches its climax, and everything comes tumbling down. Similarly, if we now think of the wider structuring of the novel, we can see that the novel is built on a whole series of opposed patterns, and that these patterns do in fact support the general tension in the novel between the disorder and chaos of the real world and the order and pattern of the world of art.

One of the most obvious of the various patterns in the novel arises from the basic contrast between the upper and the lower classes. This in turn is a part of the contrast between the usual band of good characters we can expect to encounter in a Dickens novel (such as Sol Gills, Cap'n Cuttle, Walter, Florence, Polly Toodle and co.), and a separate band of greedy, pretentious and affected characters (such as Dombey, Carker, Bagstock and Mrs Skewton). It is important to remember, too, that this is a contrast which allows for ironic comment to be made. We have already noted, for example, how Florence's home is paralleled by Walter's, and how this is done ironically: Florence's home, which should be that of a real family, is actually devoid of love, whereas the orphaned Walter's home is one of warmth and natural affection. This parallel goes much further: the rise in the fortunes of the house of Dombey parallels the fall in fortune of Sol Gills's nautical shop, while later, as Dombey's firm collapses, old Sol's fortunes begin rapidly to increase. This in turn ties in with the general conflict in the novel between love and money, and between commercial considerations on the one hand and a generosity of spirit on the other. For example, when Dombey's firm collapses, he is deserted by Bagstock, Carker and polite society generally. Sol Gills, however, finding himself penniless and in Barbados, is able to return home by virtue of the generosity of spirit of himself and his old seafaring friends: 'I found many captains and others ... who had known me for years, and who assisted me with a passage ... and I was able to do a little in return in my own craft' (p. 894). Such parallels operate throughout the novel, and offer an ironic comment on the world of money and on the characters who are a part of that world.

Similarly, within the two camps of the good characters on the one side and the bad characters on the other, more parallels can be easily discovered. Alice and old Mrs Brown, for example, parallel Mrs Skewton and her daughter, Edith. Both mothers have hawked their daughters about in an attempt to gratify their own desire for social status and wealth. And the result of these mothers' actions has been, in both cases, to ruin their daughters. This in itself is indicative of Dickens's deep disquiet about the values of a society so motivated by the acquisition of wealth and social status. Mrs Skewton, for example, still acts out her role as the captivating 'Cleopatra' she was in her 'teens, despite the fact that she is now old and decrepit, held together by make-up, wigs and stays. The normal parent–child relationship breaks down regularly in *Dombey and Son*, and the novel is full of bad parents, from all social classes. What this suggests is that, although the upper and the lower classes are actually mutually exclusive of each other, they none the less repeat each other precisely – a point later emphasised by the discovery that Alice and Edith are in fact cousins. This in turn suggests that in *Dombey and Son* Dickens is talking not only about the corrupt values of his contemporary society, but also about something constant in human affairs, irrespective of social standing in the world.

You can go on and on like this, digging about in the novel for these parallels, and you will find that they are extremely numerous, and all interrelated. The important thing to remember is that they all feed in to the development of the themes at the centre of the novel, and it is therefore possible to demonstrate that the basic conflict between money and love is in fact implicit in the novel's narrative structure. The way Dickens tells his story is not merely tagged on to the novel's events, but is actually inherent in it.

One of the results of this degree of internal artistic integrity, where everything fits together to the extent I have indicated above, is that we, as readers, quickly become very conscious of situations and events in the novel which not only function to produce a sense of the novel's reality, but function also in an ostentatiously artistic way. The most distinctive way in which this happens in *Dombey and Son* is through the repetition of certain phrases, sentences and patterns which draw attention to themselves simply by virtue of their repetition. Again, it would be pointless for me to cite every example of this device here, but you should, when studying the novel, have noted all such repetitions in your preliminary work, and know what to say about them. The kind of repetitions I have in mind are such things as Cap'n Cuttle's repetition of the song of 'Lovely Peg' or his 'Turn Again Whittington' phrase which he applies to young Walter. These actually comment upon the development of the novel's story: Walter will indeed, like his counterpart in 'Lovely Peg', marry the beautiful heroine of the song, who in his case becomes Florence; similarly, his fortunes will increase, just as did Dick Whittington's, who came out of obscurity to become Lord Mayor of London. Again, what we can notice here is the artistic integrity of the whole, how each piece slots into the larger structure of the novel and has its part to play.

It is equally important, however, to remember that these repetitions are not just a clever set of card-tricks; in each instance, they will develop as well as comment on the novel's central thematic concerns. If you do not remember this, then you run the risk of merely describing the novel without actually getting at its centre, and your criticism will consequently seem very dry and sterile. What you have always to do is to use your observation to help you towards a better understanding of what the novel is about.

For example, when you read *Dombey and Son*, it is impossible not to notice the number of times that watches and timepieces are mentioned, or the number of times the railway is mentioned, or the number of times the sea is mentioned – all of which figure prominently in the original frontispiece to the novel, which is reproduced in the Penguin edition. As always, before you start getting bogged down with all the details of the text and counting how many times each of these occurs, it is worth thinking about these things in the broadest possible terms.

From the very opening of the novel, watches and clocks recur with their own clockwork regularity: the clock Paul imagines is talking to him at Dr Blimber's; the 'very loud ticking watch' (p. 51) the young Florence associates with her father; the ticking watch of the doctors at the death of Mrs Dombey, and of the doctor who looks after Paul at Dr Blimber's; Sol Gills's perfectly accurate chronometer; the watch Cuttle winds up and gives to Walter when he leaves.

This is clearly no whim on Dickens's part. If you recall the first few paragraphs of the novel, you will remember that Time entered there personified, and accompanied by Mr Dombey, who 'jingled and jingled [his] heavy gold watch-chain' (p. 49). What is significant here is that time is being presented in two quite different ways. On the one hand, Time is personified, representative of the larger, general sweep of time in the cosmic sense; on the other, Mr Dombey's watch is representative of time in the narrower, mechanical sense. Clocks, watches and timepieces are all obviously symbolic of the mechanisation of life, and of things running to order. Time, on the other hand, which is a more general, abstract concept, has to do with the larger movement of time, with mortality and the eternal sweep of existence. So we can suggest that the imagery of clocks and watches serves two related but quite different ideas: the idea of the increasing mechanisation of life on the one hand, thoughts of mortality and of the nature of life and death on the other. Or, at least, that for the moment is what the symbol seems to suggest. These two ideas find a focus in two further symbols which reside at the centre of the novel: the railway and the sea.

Literary-critical acrobatics are not required to understand how the symbols of the railway and the sea fit in with the ideas I have been sketching out above. The railway is itself symbolic of a society running to order, to fixed timetables – just as Mr Dombey plots out in his own mind Paul's future and the future he will bring to the firm of *Dombey and Son*. Opposed to this is the natural timepiece of which the sea is symbolic, and which, in the event, frustrates all of Dombey's worldly plans when Paul dies. What this contrast suggests is not only that human society is becoming mechanical in soul as well as in body, but that there is a fundamental conflict between the two types of time, simply because time in the abstract sense cuts straight across all the details and planning of whatever timetables humans may devise.

Even so, and despite these semi-philosophical differences, the idea of the railway as being somehow representative of time does in fact seem to fit in with the general symbolic movement of the novel. We can see this in that the railway is commonly associated with and personified as Death. It is, of course, a railway train which eventually kills Carker, but the idea is foreshadowed very much earlier in the novel, as in the following passage, which describes Dombey's thoughts on the train taking him from London to Leamington shortly after Paul's death:

> Through the hollow, on the height, by the heath, by the orchard, by the park, by the garden, over the canal, across the river, where the sheep are feeding, where the mill is going, where the barge is floating, where the dead are lying, where the factory is smoking, where the stream is running, where the village clusters, where the great cathedral rises, where the bleak moor lies, and the wild breeze smoothes or ruffles it at its inconstant will; away, with a shriek, and a roar, and a rattle, and no trace to leave behind but dust and vapour: like as in the track of the remorseless monster, Death!   (p. 354)

The first thing we can say about this extract is what a brilliant piece of writing it is. It is one of those passages which, when you are reading the novel, you just have to read a second and probably third time before you continue. The passage stops you. This is because it is a very strange piece of writing to find in a novel, and it is therefore obtrusive, drawing our attention to it.

One of the reasons why this passage is so obtrusive is that it is using language in a very much more heightened way than the normally descriptive prose we associate with the novel. The way in which the passage piles phrases and clauses one upon another ('by the heath, by the orchard, by the park, by the garden', 'where the sheep are feeding, where the mill is going, where the barge is floating'), is very much more reminiscent of the language and technique of poetry than it is of prose. Indeed, the phrases and clauses are of a regular and recurring syllabic and metrical length ('by the heath, by the orchard, by the park, by the garden', etc.), and this produces a perfect tie between form and function; the beat of the writing actually imitates the sound and movement of the train itself, and this technique is a characteristic of poetry. The result is to draw our attention to the power of art to order and pattern the real world, since we know that the real world never arranges itself as neatly as it is described here. This suggests that, as we have seen earlier, the novel is offering some kind of discussion about the relationship between art and life, since it so overtly contrasts literary neatness with life's lack of such neat patterns.

Such a reading is supported by the thematic concerns of the novel as a whole. Immediately preceding this passage, Dombey meets by chance with Toodle, the engine-driver, and notes with disapproval that this 'coarse churl' (p. 353) had the presumption to be wearing a piece of black crepe in his cap-band, in memory of the recently dead Paul, Dombey's son. And this in turn forces Dombey to notice the relentless power of death to visit all classes of society, irrespective of wealth or social standing, and irrespective, too, of Dombey's plans. Similarly, if we now look again at the passage, we notice that ordinary human life is still going on: the mill is 'going', the factory 'smoking', and so on; but people are strangely absent. People are implied in the scene, but the only ones referred to specifically are 'the dead'. This has the effect of suggesting something to us of Dombey's state of mind, since he sees the signs of human activity all around him, and yet is curiously isolated from living people. This in turn takes us back to the darker side not only of human existence, but also of the human mind, since the passage provides us with a very powerful sense of the irrationality of Dombey's mind set against the continuity and order we see in the signs of human habitation and activity as these are described in the passage.

The above passage, then, operates on many levels simultaneously, ties in to the development of various aspects of the novel generally, and tells us something too, of the darker side of Dickens's imagination. Perhaps the central thing to get hold of, however, is the way in which the symbol of the railway seems to unify so many aspects of the novel. The railway links all classes of society (Toodle drives it, Dombey is a passenger), and, functioning as a symbol of Death, similarly links all classes of society, since death is singularly free of prejudice in its choice of victim. Likewise, the train, which takes Dombey to Leamington and ultimately to his ruin (through his disastrous marriage to Edith and Carker's consequent betrayal), is what eventually destroys Carker himself, while Dombey is saved by Florence's love. In many ways, then, it can be said that the symbol of the railway serves to pull together many aspects of the novel, producing a unified symbolic structure.

Or does it?

To my mind, there has always been something very unsatisfactory about the symbolism surrounding the railway. For one thing, it is so extremely obtrusive in the passages in which it occurs. Paragraphs overtly imitative of the above passage recur endlessly, banging away resolutely, but never seeming really to add to our understanding. In the chapter in which Carker is killed, for example, there are no fewer than nine passages like the above before he is eventually run down by the train. This excessive and obtrusive repetition seems to suggest some straining on Dickens's part to load certain things with some kind of transcendent meaning. But it is difficult to discover the precise nature of that meaning, simply because the transcendental qualities of Death are not easily reconciled with the reality of the train being driven by Toodle and rattling its way over the landscape of the novel. Furthermore, if we again look back to the last passage I analysed, we can discover something of the unsatisfactory aspect of the novel's symbolic structure actually evident in the details of the text.

As I pointed out, the passage gains much of its effect through its building of repeated phrases and clauses one upon another. Yet it is when the pattern breaks down that it becomes most noticeable, as here: 'where the great cathedral rises, where the bleak moor lies, and the wild breeze smoothes or ruffles it at its inconstant will', where the last clause disrupts the established pattern and brings things to a sudden stop. Stopping the passage so abruptly immediately foregrounds what it is that breaks the pattern: 'and the wild breeze smoothes or ruffles it at its will'. This 'wild breeze' is clearly significant, since our attention is drawn to it, but what does it represent?

The first thing we can notice about it is that it is 'wild' and implicitly therefore unconstrained. This is in direct contrast to the railway, which runs to time and on laid-down tracks. Now, this seems to suggest that the railway is being likened to Dombey's plans for Paul, which were equally ordered, but which were cut across by the 'inconstant' and quite arbitrary attentions of Death. So, therefore, the 'wild' and 'inconstant' breeze is symbolic here of Death, which ruined all Dombey's plans. But just one moment: previously, the *railway* was symbolic of Death. Clearly, there is something deeply wrong here; it simply does not make artistic sense to have two symbols for the same thing, one of which is running to order, and the other of which is 'wild' and unconstrained. And this leads me to detect a fundamental confusion in the novel's symbolic structuring. When looked at in detail, the text simply does not support any coherent structure, and despite the fact that in the broad panorama of the novel we are aware that some kind of symbolic structure seems to exist.

The unsatisfactory aspect of the novel's symbolic structure is equally apparent when we consider its other major symbol: the sea. After the death of Mrs Skewton, for example, we find the following:

> So Edith's mother lies unmentioned of her dear friends, who are deaf to the waves that are hoarse with repetition of their mystery, and blind to the dust that is piled upon the shore, and to the white arms that are beckoning, in the moonlight, to the invisible country far away. But all goes on, as it was wont, upon the margin of the unknown sea; and Edith standing there alone, and listening to its waves, has dank weed cast up at her feet, to strew her path in life withal. (pp. 675–6)

By this point in the novel, we have come to understand that the sea is symbolic of the other side of time to which I have referred above: the cosmic and the universal. And certainly the sea, like the railway, does at first seem wholly appropriate to the novel's symbolic structure. Florence's mother, who dies in the first chapter of the novel, drifts out 'upon the dark and unknown sea that rolls round all the world' (p. 60); the sickly Paul, pushed in his wheelchair by the old salt, Glubb, listens to 'what the waves are saying' (p. 171); Dombey's trade as a merchant is necessarily dependent upon his ships and the sea; Walter is sent off to Barbados on the ironically named *Son and Heir*; Cap'n Cuttle and Sol Gills are both associated with the sea. But, when we consider precisely how the sea works as a symbol, we are again left with a sense that it is unsatisfactorily developed.

In the above passage, for example, we are neither sure what the sea symbolises nor particularly affected by that symbol. The sea is first personified as being 'hoarse with repetition' and beckoning with 'white arms'. And yet what it repeats, and from where it is beckoning, is first 'a mystery', and secondly 'an invisible country far away'. There is no precision either in the writing or in the imaginative and symbolic pattern within which the passage should be working. Instead, the writing degenerates into loose and vapid imprecision. The world goes on, we are told, 'as it was wont' – a monstrous enough archaism even in Dickens's day. Similarly, Edith is described as standing 'with dank weed cast up at her feet, to strew her path in life withal'. It is difficult to understand how it is that a writer of Dickens's genius can lapse into this clutter of meaningless drivel and cliché. But, as always, it is our job as critics to seek an explanation for it, an explanation which fits in with a coherent overall sense of the novel, and is supported by the evidence of the text itself.

First of all, just as it is difficult to reconcile the railway as a symbol with the railway in the context of the novel's reality, so it is equally difficult to reconcile our sense of the sea as a symbol with all the novel's characters and events associated with it. That is, because we are never quite sure what transcendent 'mystery' the sea either whispers or is symbolic of, so it is impossible to conceive of it as separate from the real sea with which such characters as Cap'n Cuttle, old Glubb, Bunsby and Sol Gills are associated. Furthermore, as we saw in the above passage, when Dickens comes to the point where he needs to offer us some sense of symbolic precision about the sea, he retreats instead into archaism and cliché.

There are various ways in which we can begin to account for this. Some critics may argue that, because Dickens was writing to strict deadlines, it is understandable if parts of his narrative lapse occasionally. This would be all very well if these lapses were occasional, but the point I want to make is that the symbolic structure of the novel (particularly that concerning the railway and the sea) is *fundamentally* inconsistent and imprecise. For example, if you think back to the point I was making about the two types of time to which Dickens seems to be drawing our attention (the mechanical and ordered as opposed to the cosmic and the universal), it is very difficult to separate those in our minds, although it is clear that the text is motioning toward the idea that these two types of time are indeed quite different. But how are they different? At the point when the novel needs to elucidate this to us (as in the scene describing Dombey's thoughts on the train to Leamington), we have instead only confusion, with the 'wild' breeze and the railway suddenly both becoming symbolic of Death. This fundamental confusion is, I believe, the key to why the symbolic structure of *Dombey and Son* is so unsatisfactory. In *Dombey and Son*, Dickens is motioning toward another area of human experience, an area which language may ultimately be unable to express. And this is precisely why Dickens is forced to retreat into platitudes and structural confusions when he is closest to that unknown area; simply because language may be capable of motioning toward it, but finally incapable of expressing it.

Such a reading is well supported by evidence from the text. The following scene, for example, occurs at Sol Gills's, just before Walter is to leave for Barbados. There has been a good deal of emotion revealed already, with Florence, near to tears, craving old Sol's kind indulgence that he might allow her to be his very bestest, bestest friend while Walter is away, so that they might care for each other. Old Sol agrees with heart-rending honesty, while Susan Nipper, who has accompanied Florence, impatiently leaned back 'with her arms crossed ... bit one end of her bonnet strings, and heaved a gentle sigh as she looked up at the skylight' (p. 335). Susan Nipper's apparent impatience with the scene before her (for which her bonnet strings suffer considerably) is continued in the scene which immediately follows:

> It seemed to him [Walter] that he responded to her [Florence's] innocent appeal, beside the dead child's bed: and, in the solemn presence he had seen there, pledged himself to cherish and protect her very image in his banishment, with brotherly regard; to garner up her simple faith, inviolate; and hold himself degraded if he breathed upon it any thought that was not in her own breast when she gave it to him.
>
> Susan Nipper, who had bitten both her bonnet strings at once, and imparted a great deal of private emotion to the skylight, during this transaction, now changed the subject by inquiring who took milk and who took sugar; and being enlightened on these points, poured out the tea.   (p. 337)

It is not difficult to see in this passage the way in which Dickens ironically undercuts himself. The first paragraph is painfully reminiscent of the previous passage, in which the sea figured so mysteriously. In fact, it is more than merely reminiscent, since it is almost parodic of the style of writing we do in fact find in many of the lesser-rate Victorian novelists. The whole paragraph is just a string of gushy phrases which it is impossible to read in any way other than parody: Florence's appeal is 'innocent', her presence 'solemn'; Walter 'pledges himself' to 'cherish and protect her very image', to 'garner up her simple faith, inviolate'. And so it goes on.

The second paragraph adds to our sense of the parody of

emotion we see being played out before us. Susan Nipper, who had 'bitten both her bonnet strings at once, and imparted a good deal of emotion to the skylight', suddenly changes the subject by inquiring 'who took milk and who took sugar; and being enlightened on these points, poured out the tea'. This is the final irony of the extract, precisely undercutting the flights of emotion of Walter and Florence. There simply is nothing so mundane, so everyday and humdrum that could possibly contrast more strongly with Walter and Florence's tear-jerking declarations than Susan's interest in the making of tea. There is everything to suggest here that Dickens is quite aware of the impossibility of presenting the emotion that actually motivates these characters, and that he consciously parodies any attempt to do so.

But what this further suggests is Dickens's sense of dissatisfaction with language, and even, perhaps, with the novel as a form capable of probing or exploring those hidden areas of human experience. To follow this idea a little further, you might like to look at the scene between Paul and Mr Toots, in which Paul is talking about whatever it is the sea keeps whispering to him, and the mysterious boat he has seen beckoning to him. Toots, steadfastly literal to the end, imagines it must be 'Smugglers', but, 'with an impartial remembrance of there being two sides to every question', he added 'or Preventive' (p. 337). In this scene, as in the above extract, we have a strong sense that Dickens is consciously undercutting himself precisely at the moment when he most needs to elucidate with the greatest precision exactly what it is he is talking about. It is my belief that a writer of Dickens's genius would have elucidated it with more precision if it had been possible. That he does not indicates that it simply is not possible in the form of the novel in which Dickens was writing.

What this also suggests is that in *Dombey and Son* Dickens creates, as he does in several other of the novels I have considered in this book, two stories. In the parts of the novel describing Dombey, Carker, Mrs Skewton, Bagstock and Edith he presents social life and human beings as cruel, complicated and unjust, motivated by greed and affectation. But in the parts of his story concerned with Florence and Walter, Sol Gills and Cap'n Cuttle he presents a far more palatable and purposeful story in which characters are good, just, and motivated by a simple generosity of spirit and love for their fellow humans. This is the world as Dickens would like it to be, but it is not meant to be convincing.

Florence, for example, has every reason to despise both Paul and her father; instead, she swamps them both with love. We all know that this is not how a girl in Florence's position would behave; Florence is simply too good to be true. But that, of course, is precisely the point, because she is not *meant* to be true. This is emphasised by the fact that the story in which she plays her major part is a mixture of two fairy-tales: Dick Whittington and Cinderella. But fairy-tales, like Florence and all the other good characters in *Dombey and Son,* are untrue. Consequently, as we have seen at various points in this chapter, it can be argued that in *Dombey and Son* Dickens is playing with the notion of imposing fictional patterns upon the chaos of the world; or, in other words, he is setting the disorder of life against the fantasy order of art.

Or, at least, that is the conclusion I draw. And, it is a conclusion I draw *purely from the evidence of the text.* Your analysis of the evidence of the text might lead you to draw quite different conclusions, and that is, indeed, the whole point of this book. It is your argument and your response to the novel which is the most important thing, supported, as it must always be, by evidence from the text. This will of course take time as you will have to ponder over the passages you select for analysis, but it will be time well spent. A critical book can only provide you with someone else's view of a novel, but if you look at the text for yourself you can't help but develop your own ideas. In addition, as the next chapter explains, you will be acquiring a stock of material that you can use directly and effectively in essays.

7

Writing an essay

ONE OF the things that makes studying English unlike studying any other subject is that success depends upon your ability to write a good essay. Tell yourself from the start, therefore, that you are going to produce really good essays, essays that examiners will want to praise rather than find fault with. If you haven't yet discovered a method of essay-writing for yourself, what I can do here is to steer you toward a productive approach.

It all starts with appreciating what you are trying to do in an essay. This can be summed up in a simple formula: *in a critical essay you are trying to build a clear argument from the evidence of the text*. The method of your essay should be equally simple. But before you start you need to understand the question and you need to know roughly what shape your answer is going to take. This doesn't mean knowing 'the answer' to the question from the out-set, but it does mean knowing how many paragraphs you are going to write and roughly how long they are going to be.

The rest of this chapter explains all of this more fully, but it might be a good idea if I summarise the main points here at the outset just to get across the idea of how simple the method of a good essay can, and indeed should, be. Recognise that you are being asked a question and that this means you will have to argue an answer. There is no sense in trying to give your complete answer in the first paragraph of the essay; if you do, you won't have any other points to make or go on to, and you will almost certainly tie yourself up in knots by trying to say too much at once. *Use your first paragraph just to clarify what the issue is that you are being asked to consider.*

Once you have got to grips with the question, there is only one place to find the answer: in the text. So, *start your second para-graph by turning to a specific scene to analyse.* Try to establish something central to the question from this scene. When you have done this, you can conclude the paragraph, and proceed to another paragraph, and so on. *Build your essay in paragraph blocks, making each paragraph establish a step in a logical argument.* By the time you have looked at five or six episodes, and discussed them in the light of the question you are considering, a clear argument should have developed. And you will have achieved the aim of an essay: you will have built a clear argument from the evidence of the text. The rest of this chapter repeats this advice at greater length, making reference to a specific question.

The question

Teachers and examiners set questions; most students fail to answer the questions set. That might seem absurd but it is true. Asked a specific question about Dombey in *Dombey and Son,* most examination candidates will just pour out everything they know about him. So, make sure that you answer the question set. In order to do this, you need to realise that questions confront you with something to discuss. Take this example of a question on *Dombey and Son*:

To what extent do the characters in *Dombey and Son* remain constant as their circumstances change?

There is no single correct answer to this question. You could argue that they do change, or that they remain constant, or that some of them change. But the very fact that different views can be taken should make it clear that you will have to argue a case in your answer, proving that case from your reading of the evidence of the text.

Another thing to grasp is that there is no such thing as an easy question or a difficult question. The question I have given here might seem relatively simple, and this can deceive students into thinking that their answers can be loose and chatty. The point to realise about questions, however, is that they are always asking you about the central issues in the novel. In order to help you organise your answer the examiner selects a particular aspect of the work – in this instance the characters – and you must concentrate on this aspect, but your answer must be informed by a larger sense of the work. This might seem difficult, but it's not: all the earlier chapters of this book have stressed the importance of seeing a broad pattern in a novel. This is what I mean here by 'a larger sense of the work'. In this question on *Dombey and Son,* you are being asked to consider whether *the nature of the characters* changes *as their social circumstances* change. If, as in this example, you can see that the question reflects the larger money-*versus*-love opposition in Dickens's novels, then this will give your answer a sense of direction and purpose: you will see that the question bears on the whole subject of the novel and that more is required than just a description of the characters.

The first paragraph

If you cannot sum up the question in the way described above, don't worry. You don't need to sort everything out before you start because an essay itself should help you discover the answer. Use your first paragraph merely to define the issue involved in the question. For example, an opening paragraph might read as follows:

> In *Dombey and Son* we see dramatic changes in the lives of all the principal characters. This is most true of Mr Dombey, who at the opening of the novel is a wealthy merchant, then loses everything, and is finally left happy with Florence, the daughter he had previously neglected. But Florence's circumstances change greatly, too. She runs away from her wealthy home to escape her father's cruelty and eventually marries Walter Gay, who is very poor and apparently without any real prospects in the world. Similarly, the proud, genteel but penniless Edith Granger, Dombey's second wife, undergoes great changes, particularly after she runs away with James Carker, one of Mr Dombey's managers. The question, however, is whether the characters themselves change as their circumstances change. A closer look at some of their experiences should help reveal the answer.

Can you see how, in this short paragraph, I have done just enough scene-setting to make it clear what I am talking about, and have asked, but not attempted to answer, the main question? A first paragraph should be as short and to the point as this. If you find yourself rambling on it will almost certainly be the case that you are losing the thread of what you are saying, and failing to define clearly the subject of your essay.

The second paragraph

Using paragraphs effectively is probably the central secret of writing good essays. I have already talked about the need for a clear first paragraph which is to the point and gives a sense of the direction you are going to take. Each subsequent paragraph should also be disciplined and serve a purpose.

Look at it this way: in your opening paragraph you will have identified the issue for discussion; your closing paragraph will wrap things up. In between you should have about five or six paragraphs of half to two-thirds of a page in length. Each will represent a step forward in your answer to the question and make a distinct advance on the previous paragraph. If paragraphs are too short, the ideas will be skimpily expressed. If the paragraphs are too long, you will lose the thread of what you are saying. An examiner can tell a lot about an essay just by looking at its appearance: if an essay is constructed in about seven or eight paragraphs, and the five or six central paragraphs are all of a fairly similar length, then the examiner will be surprised if the answer is disappointing, as such a clear layout virtually guarantees clear thinking.

As your second paragraph begins, turn to the text. A second paragraph on the question we are using might begin, 'We first learn something of the character of Mr Dombey at the very opening of the novel, immediately after the birth of his son, Paul.' In the course of this book I have quoted fairly lengthy extracts from novels, but obviously this is not practical in an essay. What is practical, however, is to describe vividly the incident you have in mind. After that, start to discuss what strikes you as important in the scene. What you are looking for are points relevant to the question: this early scene from *Dombey and Son,* for example, conveys a sense of how Mr Dombey seems to be motivated purely by commercial considerations, and suggests that this breeds a certain isolation in his character; but you have got to descibe how this specific scene creates this impression of the character. After referring to the text, and having discussed a scene, you will need to pull the threads of this paragraph together. This is vitally important; at the end of a paragraph you must stand back and sum up what you have established so far. With Dombey, you might review your progress and say that Dickens offers us a sense of Dombey as a very proud and arrogant personality, motivated purely by commercial considerations, and that this engenders in him a certain isolation from other characters, since he is unable to share in any natural and emotional contact with them. The passage examined, therefore, has established something about the nature of this man.

Always make sure that you do sum up at the end of a paragraph in this way, forcing yourself to write two or three sentences of conclusion. This will ensure that you are answering the question, and will help push along an argument in your essay. The concluding sentences should also trigger off your next paragraph. For example, the logical starting-place for our next paragraph on Dombey would be that, having seen the strength of his personality, we want to see whether he changes as the novel progresses. And the way to find out is to choose a scene from later in the novel which looks as if it will help you answer the question.

I hope it is clear how the method described here can be used for any question about Dickens: the approach to take at all times is to build your argument from the evidence of the text. Another relevant point to remember is that an essay should be self-sufficient. You are trying to persuade the reader of your essay, trying to convince the examiner. Consequently, it serves no purpose whatsoever to say something like 'the incident on page 143 proves that ...'. A page reference proves nothing; you have got to convey a sense of the text, so that the reader of the essay feels that he or she is confronting the evidence from which you are drawing your conclusions. This might also be a good place to mention style. Quite simply, don't worry about it. If you are conveying a vivid sense of the text and then making your points clearly and logically, then your style will be equally vivid and persuasive.

What you must worry about, however, is writing in grammatical sentences. Nobody expects every sentence to be perfect, but a sentence that rambles on and on won't make sense. All of this is largely a matter of thinking about what you are doing: it is better to think about what a sentence says rather than gabbling out sentences as quickly as possible. People only write badly when they don't think what they are saying and don't order their thoughts.

The third paragraph

Each paragraph should trigger off the direction in which you head in the next paragraph, so in *Dombey and Son,* searching for a scene where Dombey is at the centre of things, you might choose the episode in which Dombey delivers his ultimatum to Edith, in the company of Carker. Again describe the scene, then comment on everything in it that strikes you as relevant to the question. You might be able to remember certain phrases or particular details about the scene: it is the way in which you make use of these that will really bring your essay to life. In this scene, for example, you could make a great deal out of how Carker seems to be embarrassed by the open conflict between Dombey and his wife, but is in fact watching very carefully for each character's weak points like a cat, ready to pounce when the opportunity occurs. Then, at the end of the paragraph, again devote two or three sentences to pulling the threads together and drawing a conclusion. What you might decide about Dombey, for example, is that his pride and arrogance, which prevents him from having any real relationship with Edith, also makes him blind to Carker's calculated plans. As your answer progresses, providing you take care to sum up at the end of each paragraph, you should discover that you are getting hold of the larger issues of the novel. What you might realise by this stage is that characters are trapped by money into behaving in a quite unnatural and affected way in order to present an acceptable front to society. This is the point I have made throughout this book, that the world of money actively poisons and frustrates any natural relationship between characters.

Continuing to build

The questions to ask yourself at the start of each paragraph are, 'Is there another aspect to this question that I have not considered yet?' and 'Is this the whole story, or is there something that contradicts what I have said so far?' Consequently, answering our question on *Dombey and Son,* at this stage you might decide to look at a passage which shows how Dombey changes after the loss of his fortunes. This will again demonstrate how you are getting hold of the larger issues of the novel, since he is able to love Florence only after he has lost all his money. Or you might decide to go on and consider some of the other characters. I shall pursue the second of these options here. You might consider Edith: select a suitable scene and describe it. What does the scene tell you about Edith? You might, in the same paragraph, look briefly at another scene to see if she changes. That is quite all right: you don't need to stick rigidly to a 'one scene to a paragraph' format. But do be sure that you draw the threads together at the end of the paragraph: for example, you might decide that the novel presents Edith as a haughty, proud woman, and, even though she does have a warmer side to her nature (as seen in her love for Florence), she never really alters because, to some extent, she does not have the economic freedom to change. It doesn't matter if you want to modify this reading of Edith later in your essay. The important thing is that you end your paragraph with a conclusion that sums up your impression so far: be careful never to end a paragraph with a quotation. You have always got to come in at the end of a paragraph and establish your control of the argument.

In the fifth paragraph of your essay you might consider Florence. Look at the evidence: you might intuitively feel that Florence does not change, but it is very important that you look at the evidence of the text and decide for yourself. I think the kind of conclusion I might reach, but only after looking closely at a scene or two, is that Florence's love for her father remains constant, but that she changes inasmuch as she comes to realise that love is not a one-sided affair. She learns that it is not her fault if her father cannot love her, but a failing in him, even if the cause of it is the inhumanity of the society in which he lives.

Changing direction

It can sometimes be a good idea to try and change the direction of your essay about two-thirds of the way through. In the case of our sample question you might have devoted four paragraphs to building the idea that Dickens presents a view of human nature as poisoned by the world of money. But it will add interest to your essay, and probably do more justice to the novel, if, about two-thirds of the way through, you suggest that the issue is more complicated than this. What in effect is happening is that the earlier stages of your answer have established a broad view of the novel, but now, in the last third, you can start to look for complications in the text. That might at first seem a bit difficult to understand, but your argument so far does actually move you in this direction anyway. The following paragraph shows you how you can change direction in the way I mean.

As always, start by picking a scene. A good one to use here would be the description of Dombey the evening after he has returned with Edith from honeymoon. In this scene, Florence has unusually been allowed to take her sewing into Dombey's room. Dombey is apparently dozing, a newspaper covering his face. In fact, he is awake, watching Florence at her work. When Edith enters, he witnesses, unobserved, the natural affection between the two women, and this arouses a variety of conflicting emotions in him, ranging from jealousy to a deep desire to force Edith to show him the same affection she shows Florence, and to a sad recognition that he is emotionally isolated from them both. What this suggests is that in *Dombey and Son* characters such as Mr Dombey are caught between the pull of finer instincts and the sort of self-interest and desire to dominate other people that is likely to be encouraged by the inhumane society in which they live. This means that you can make a much more elaborate argument about how characters change in *Dombey and Son* than you would just by noting that some of them do change. We know Dombey changes, and have demonstrated the extent of the change in him, but what this final shift in direction allows you to do is to suggest a conflict within the character and to show just how deeply trapped characters are by the world of money, but how, beneath the face they present to the world, there are still finer, if constrained, emotions. Working at the text in this way allows you to show a much more complicated reading of the question, but also means that in each passage you analyse you are still focusing your attention on the wider issues of the novel.

In the next paragraph you could follow up the argument about how characters are caught between the pull of finer instincts and the sort of affectation that is likely to be encouraged in a society dominated by money by suggesting that if what you have said about Dombey is true, then you should be able to discover this in other characters, too, such as Carker. A passage you could consider here might be the meeting between Edith and Carker in the French hotel apartment where they had planned to meet. What you might like to draw attention to here is the faded gentility and seediness of the hotel rooms in which they meet, and how this is indicative of Carker's sordid intentions toward Edith. Some characters, such as Carker, are so poisoned by the kind of lust, greed and affectation encouraged by the world of money that they simply cannot change. Edith, on the other hand, in refusing to become Carker's mistress, does demonstrate the pull between finer emotions and the need to survive in a society dominated by money. In finally refusing Carker she changes from being a woman dominated by the world of money to a woman able to make her own decisions. She is no longer the property of anyone else, and this represents a distinct change in her character. This allows you to demonstrate that the idea of characters changing in *Dombey and Son* is actually much more complicated than it might at first appear. Some characters, such as Dombey, although trapped by the world of money, actually have enough good in them still to change and to discover a natural relationship with other people. Others, such as Edith, finally refuse any longer to be subject to the dictates of society. Others still, however, such as Carker, will never change, since their very nature has been fundamentally blighted by the poisoning and pernicious effects of the world of money. This gives you a very different view on the idea of characters changing in the novel, and, if you can alter the direction of your argument in the last third, as I have here, then that adds a whole additional level of interest to your essay.

The concluding paragraph

You might feel a little hesitant about writing your concluding paragraph, as, having been firmly in control all along the way, there should be nothing new left to say at the end. But what will happen is that, having managed to write a really clear and well-controlled answer, you will find that the words begin to flow in this last paragraph, since all you have to do is sum up the answer to the question, the answer you have finally arrived at. But there is one thing I want to stress about your concluding paragraph, although I have mentioned it in passing already: never end your essay with a quotation. This is a very common mistake in students' essays. Having written what may be quite a good essay, students all too often spoil everything by ending with a quotation. But the examiner will have read the novel and will have worked out his or her interpretation of it, so there really is no point in just banging down a quotation as if that's the last word on the subject. That is, don't expect the novel (or the critic!) to do your job for you. The examiner will want to see what you make of the evidence you have gleaned from the text, so you must always come in at the end of your essay and finally establish your control of the argument.

Use the format of the essay to help you solve the problem

This is all very well, you might say, but the question I have to answer is far more tricky than the question considered above. The whole point of this chapter, however, is to argue that the same method will help you answer any question, and answer it really well. Indeed, this essay format should help you sort out an answer. Let us assume that you have been asked to discuss the various effects that money has on Pip in *Great Expectations.* Your first paragraph can suggest that, since *Great Expectations* tells the story of what happens to Pip when he receives money from an unknown benefactor, it can be expected that the effects of his new wealth on him will be a central concern of the novel, and that the way to discuss these effects is by looking at some of his experiences. Then, in paragraph two, look at a scene, perhaps featuring Pip in the first excitement of his new-found wealth. On the basis of this passage you should be able to establish a first point in your argument. Consideration of more scenes will then push your argument along, provided that you remember that each paragraph must advance on the paragraph before. In the last third of your essay, you might, in order to change direction, switch to consider something of how other characters manipulate him by virtue of the money they possess. Really it is a case of reducing the essay to logical steps, and then building your answer in logical steps. This is what is so good about this kind of systematic approach: it allows you the freedom to express and develop your own ideas, and convey your enjoyment and appreciation of a text. In other words, having a clear essay method allows you to be inventive and enthusiastic and original, because you know that you are building a solid and sensible argument from the evidence of the text.

Further reading

Before you start reading a lot of critical books about Dickens – indeed, before you read any critical book – ask yourself why you are bothering to do so. Critical books are useful, but only if you use them in the right way. They should complement your own thinking about a text rather than serve as a substitute for thinking. The most important thing to remember is that your criticism will only stand up if it is based on your own impressions and experience of the text. It might be that you just cannot see what a novel is about, that it leaves you totally baffled. At this point, a clear introduction to the novel which draws attention to its central themes can be very helpful. More often than not, the introductory essay in the edition of the novel you are using should prove illuminating in this kind of way. The introductions to the Penguin editions of Dickens are particularly good.

Another useful purpose these introductions serve is if you want to verify your own response; it can be very encouraging to turn to a critical essay which shows that your thinking about a novel is on the right lines. At the outset, if you are going to bother with criticism at all, don't search for unusual or eccentric criticism. What you need to establish before anything else is a clear and sensible understanding of the text. The chances are that, if you leap straight into unusual or eccentric criticism, you will become confused, and you will certainly not get a clear understanding of the novel's central themes. Good critics arrive at unusual interpretations only after spending a considerable amount of time thinking about and analysing a text, so to begin with stick to the kind of solid introductions mentioned above.

This is precisely why I have discussed the novels in the order I have in this book. At the outset, I wanted to establish the major themes at the centre of *all* Dickens's novels, and these themes are particularly explicit in *Hard Times* (1854). I then went on, looking in increasing detail at longer and more complicated novels, finishing with *Dombey and Son* (1848). Of course, this has meant that in this book I have not discussed Dickens's novels in the order in which they were published. The order in which I have considered them is that which enabled me best to illustrate, and develop, a method of looking at the novels. Nor have I looked at all the novels, although it should be apparent that the approach I have presented will work with any of Dickens's novels.

I have used the Penguin editions of Dickens's novels throughout this book, as these are often the most readily available paperbacks, but obviously any good edition (that is to say, an edition with an introduction and notes) will serve if you are studying Dickens. The Oxford University Press editions of Dickens (published in the World's Classics series) are also good. If you are reading only for pleasure, of course, even the tattiest old beaten-up edition from the local jumble sale will still convey all of Dickens's genius and magic. And that is what I hope this book has done: although I have looked at only a few of Dickens's novels, you should be able to take the *approach* I have been recommending to any of his novels. But, as I have looked at only six of the novels, and in what might at first have appeared a rather haphazard order, it seems sensible to include a chronological list of his major fiction here:

The Pickwick Papers (1837)
Oliver Twist (1838)
Nicholas Nickleby (1839)
Master Humphrey's Clock: The Old Curiosity Shop, Barnaby Rudge (1840–1)
Martin Chuzzlewit (1844)
Dombey and Son (1848)
David Copperfield (1850)
Bleak House (1853)
Hard Times (1854)
Little Dorrit (1857)
A Tale of Two Cities (1859)
Great Expectations (1861)
Our Mutual Friend (1865)
The Mystery of Edwin Drood (1870; unfinished at Dickens's death)

As you will see from this list, Dickens was a very prolific writer. In fact, the above list is only a part of his output, for he wrote dozens of short stories, about half a dozen plays, and many essays and articles. What this prodigious ouput demonstrates is what I have been trying to draw your attention to as this book has progressed: that Dickens's novels deal with all aspects of the society in which he lived. He always wrote for a mass audience, and he was interested in the same things as interested his audience: social injustice and reform, the position of women and children in society, education, work, crime, a good murder story. As I have tried to show in this book, all these interests are deeply embedded in his fiction; it is the way in which he explores them which creates the distinctive quality of a Dickens novel: a sense of the grotesque and of fantasy, of the darker impulses which motivate people, his exuberant delight in language. If you can see these interests and qualities at work in his novels, then you really are beginning to establish a solid grasp of the text.

And really, if you can see these interests and qualities in Dickens's novels, you don't need to read any more criticism. Time spent looking at and thinking about passages from a novel is time much more usefully employed than time spent reading other people's views. But it might be that, even after doing a lot of work on the novel yourself, you still want to find out more. Indeed, working closely on a text might stimulate your interest to the point where you want to see how other people respond to the novel. This is the point at which it can prove useful to turn to criticism in order to add to or unsettle your ideas. The two times at which it is most useful to look at criticism, therefore, are just after reading the novel, when you might need some help in sorting out your general ideas and in establishing the novel's central themes, and after you have done a lot of your own work on a text, when you feel that your own thinking might benefit from some additional stimulus.

There are several books and articles I can recommend which will help you get hold of the central themes and interests of Dickens's novels. One book you will find helpful in this way is J. Hillis Miller's *Charles Dickens: The World of His Novels* (Harvard University Press, 1958). Similarly, Barbara Hardy's *The Moral Art of Dickens* (Athlone Press, 1970) presents very clearly what is central in Dickens's fiction. Once you have got hold of the central themes you might want something to stimulate your thinking. John

Carey's *The Violent Effigy: A Study of Dickens' Imagination* (Faber, 1973) is exceptionally good in this respect and will probably stop you in your tracks as you suddenly start reconsidering your view of Dickens's novels. But the important thing is: *read criticism critically*. Don't be fooled into thinking that the views of published critics are necessarily right.

A good way to balance your approach to any novelist is to read some critical books which include essays by a number of different critics. This helps you to see the variety of approaches which can be taken to a text and illustrates that all of these approaches may be in their own way quite valid. One such collection you might like to start with is *The Changing World of Charles Dickens,* edited by Robert Giddings (Vision Press, 1983). The books in the Macmillan Casebook series are also helpful here. The central one is *Dickens,* edited by A. E. Dyson (Macmillan, 1968) and this is supported by Casebooks collecting criticism on individual novels.

But, as you will soon find out when you start looking along the shelves of your library, Dickens has attracted a huge amount of critical attention. The first thing to remember is that you can't read all of it. And, even if for some perverse reason you did read all the criticism you could find on Dickens, this wouldn't necessarily guarantee that you would understand his novels any better. So, as I have already said, read critical books critically. That's all very well, you might be thinking, but how do I know if a critical book is any good? Well, first of all, have a look at the books I have recommended above. These should help you get to grips with a novel by sending you back to it to test out some new ideas. And that really is as good a way as any of judging the quality of any critical book you read: see if it sends you back to the text to explore it further for yourself.